W9-BBA-754

THE UNIVERSITY OF MICHIGAN
CENTER FOR CHINESE STUDIES

MICHIGAN MONOGRAPHS IN CHINESE STUDIES
NO. 46

CHINA'S UNIVERSITIES

Post-Mao Enrollment Policies and Their Impact on the Structure of Secondary Education

A Research Report

by
Suzanne Pepper

Ann Arbor
Center for Chinese Studies
The University of Michigan
1984

Library of Congress Cataloging in Publication Data

Pepper, Suzanne, 1900-

China's universities.

(Michigan monographs in Chinese studies; no. 46)

Includes bibliographical references.

1. Universities and colleges—China—Admission. 2. Universities and colleges—China—Entrance requirements. 3. Education, Secondary—China—Curricula. I. Title. II. Series.

LB2351.4,C6P47 1984 378'.1057'0951 83-25277

ISBN 0-89264-050-2

ISBN 0-89264-046-4 (pbk.)

Printed in the United States of America

CONTENTS

CHINESE NEWSPAPERS AND PERIODICALS CITED IN THE TEXT

National Press

Guangming ribao [Guangming daily], Beijing
Renmin ribao [People's daily], Beijing
Zhongguo qingnian bao [China youth news], Beijing

Provincial and Municipal Press

Beijing ribao [Peking daily]
Dagongbao [Ta kungpao], Hong Kong
Dazhong ribao [Public daily], Jinan, Shandong
Fujian ribao [Fujian daily], Fuzhou
Guangzhou ribao [Canton daily], Guangzhou
Nanfang ribao [South China daily], Guangzhou
Sichuan ribao [Sichuan daily], Chengdu
Tianjin ribao [Tianjin daily]
Wenhuibao [Wen weipo], Hong Kong
Wenhuibao [Wenhui news], Shanghai
Xinhua ribao [New China daily], Nanjing, Jiangsu
Yangcheng wanbao [Canton evening news], Guangzhou
Zhejiang ribao [Zhejiang daily], Hangzhou

National Journals

Hongqi [Red flag], Beijing
Jiaoxue yu yanjiu [Teaching and research], Beijing
Jiaoyu yanjiu [Education research], Beijing
Renmin jiaoyu [People's education], Beijing
Zhongguo qingnian [Chinese youth], Beijing
Zhonghua renmin gongheguo guowuyuan gongbao [Bulletin of the State Council of the People's Republic of China], cited hereafter as *State Council Bulletin*, Beijing

English Translation Services

Peking Review and *Beijing Review*, Beijing

Xinhua News Bulletin, New China News Agency, Hong Kong

Foreign Broadcast Information Service: Daily Report, People's Republic of China, cited hereafter as FBIS, United States Government, Washington, D.C.

Joint Publications Research Service, China Report, cited hereafter as *JPRS*, United States Government, Washington, D.C.

Summary of World Broadcasts, the Far East, cited hereafter as SWB, British Broadcasting Corporation monitoring service, Reading, England

PREFACE

This is the second in a series of reports on China's universities based on a 1980 research trip to China sponsored by the Committee on Scholarly Communication with the People's Republic of China (CSCPRC).[1] The visit covered a total of fourteen weeks during the spring and autumn semesters and entailed extensive interviews at a dozen universities. Due to the sensitive nature of the subject, the project had to be carefully drawn. I therefore visited only the best, or "keypoint" *(zhongdian)*, universities and, as agreed upon in advance, confined my questions to current developments, avoiding both the controversial 1966-76 decade and overtly political matters of the present. To serve as the basis for the interviews, I drew up a lengthy questionnaire covering most aspects of university life with specific reference to the 1976-80 period. The largest single block of questions concerned university enrollment and the composition of student bodies. The responses to these questions constitute the primary focus of this monograph.

The Chinese Ministry of Education, which was the direct overseer of the project, forwarded copies of my questionnaire to the selected universities prior to my arrival. The questions were usually answered by middle-level university administrators. At only two universities did I have substantive interviews with university vice-presidents, their role elsewhere being confined largely to ceremonial functions. Even at these two institutions, the vice-presidents' comments were made at the more general policy level; it was left to lower-level personnel to respond to the details of most of the questions. At one other university, I interviewed the heads of two academic departments. In all other instances, interviews were conducted with the heads, their deputies, or other personnel from the universities' administrative offices.

These offices vary marginally from one university to another but usually include the following or the equivalent thereof: the president's office *(xiaozhang bangongshi)*; the foreigners' office *(waishi bangongshi)*; the personnel office *(renshichu)*, usually including within it a student section *(xueshengke)*; the teaching affairs office *(jiaowuchu)*; the scientific research office *(kexue yanjiuchu)*, often including within it a graduate student affairs section *(yanjiushengke)*; the library *(tushuguan)*; the general affairs office *(zongwuchu)*; the financial affairs office *(caiwuchu)*, the functions of which are sometimes performed by a section within the general affairs office; and the basic construction office *(jiben jianshechu)*. Often included in the interviews as well were representatives of the Communist Youth League (CYL), the Students' Association, and the employees' union.

In all but four universities, interviews were arranged with representatives from most of the university offices and organizations listed above, totaling between ten and twenty administrators per university. With one not very successful exception, my contacts with students and faculty, both Chinese and foreign, were entirely informal and not part of the interview procedure.

The Education Ministry clearly gave the universities the option to receive me or not as they chose. As a result, my reception by the universities varied widely, from two which essentially declined to participate in the project to four which went out of their way to cooperate. Similarly, no discernible pattern emerged to reveal clearly taboo topics, with the already mentioned exceptions of the Cultural Revolution decade and the internal political workings of the universities which were clearly out of bounds in virtually all respects. Someone thus answered almost every item on the questionnaire and many more besides, since the questions grew in number and depth as the interviews progressed. But no single university answered all the questions. With respect to my queries on university enrollment, two schools, including one that was otherwise among the most cooperative, declined outright to grant interviews on any aspect of the subject. Yet these same questions were among those answered most fully by several universities.

I selected in advance and at random the universities visited, the randomness being due in part to faulty preparatory communications and uncertainty as to the nature and status of the project until it was about to commence. As a result, the selection is representative of the key universities only in terms of their geography. It omits the most prestigious among them, namely, Beijing and Qinghua universities and the Chinese Science and Technology University at Hefei. Nor does the selection contain a representative sample of China's professional and technological institutions of higher learning. The schools visited were primarily comprehensive universities *(zonghexing daxue)* which offer a combined general science *(li-ke)* and liberal arts *(wen-ke)* curriculum. The list of universities visited is as follows:

Beijing Teachers' Training University (16-17 April 1980)

Chinese People's University, Beijing (14 April)

East China (formerly Shanghai) Teachers' Training University (22-28 November)

Fudan University, Shanghai (17-21 November)

Jiangxi Communist Labor University (since renamed Jiangxi Agricultural University), Nanchang (25 October-1 November), including the Nancheng County Communist Labor Branch School (29-30 October)

Jilin University, Changchun (20-24 April)

Jilin Teachers' Training University (since renamed Northeast Teachers' Training University), Changchun (23 April)
Lanzhou University (3-8 May), including the Lanzhou Northwest National Minorities Institute (7 May)
Nanjing University (10-14 November)
Nankai University, Tianjin (26-29 April), including the Nankai University Branch School (28 April)
Shandong University, Jinan (29 November-5 December)
Sichuan University, Chengdu (12-16 May)
Wuhan University (4-7 November)
Xiamen University (18-22 October)
Zhongshan University (11 December).

With two exceptions, all of the universities listed above are national "keypoint" institutions run directly by the Ministry of Education. Of the two exceptions, one school was in the process of being demoted from that status while the other was being promoted. The Jiangxi Communist Labor University was among the eighty-eight schools designated as national keypoints (not all of which are run by the Education Ministry) when the list was first announced in 1978. This university is no longer run directly from the center; it is now under provincial control and enrolls only within Jiangxi. An Education Ministry spokesman claimed, moreover, that this school is no longer regarded as a national keypoint, and its name has since been changed to the Jiangxi Agricultural University. The second exception is Jilin Teachers' Training University at Changchun, since renamed the Northeast Teachers' Training University. This is one of the regional education schools now run directly by the Education Ministry. But this university has not been, as of mid-1983, designated as a national keypoint despite its promotion from provincial to central management.

According to the ministry spokesman interviewed in December 1980, there were at that time 98 officially designated national keypoint universities among the total of 675 institutions of higher learning throughout the country (these figures are constantly changing; in mid-1981 another foreign scholar was told there were 94 national key universities). These key institutions enrolled 67,000 new students in 1979, or 24 percent of the total 275,000 freshmen admitted that year.[2]

The ministry spokesman outlined a plan to create a smaller group of "keypoints among the keypoints," since the total number had grown too large for the center to manage in the manner intended. It had therefore been decided to select a few which could be treated as "real" keypoint universities should be, that is, as schools where the very best teachers, students, and material resources are concentrated in order to achieve more rapid development. A similar contraction was then under way nationwide among keypoint schools at the secondary and primary levels as well.

Presumably, this smaller list of universities will more or less duplicate the list of twenty-six universities singled out as the recipients of the first World Bank loan to China. Administrators at several universities identified their schools as among those scheduled to receive these funds, and although specific amounts had not yet been determined, anticipated assistance ranged from U.S. $ 1 to 3 million per school. Beijing and Qinghua universities were said to be expecting even larger amounts. All of the schools visited, with the exceptions of Jiangxi Gong-da, the Jilin Teachers' Training University, and the Chinese People's University, are on the list of those scheduled to receive the proposed World Bank assistance.[3] The following schools make up that list and provide a representative cross-section of China's leading institutions of higher learning:

Beijing University
Beijing Agricultural University
Beijing Medical College
Beijing Teachers' Training University
Central China (Huazhong) Institute of Technology, Wuhan
Chinese Science and Technology University, Hefei
Chongqing University
Dalian Institute of Technology
East China (Huadong) Teachers' Training University, Shanghai
Fudan University, Shanghai
Jilin University, Changchun
Lanzhou University
Nanjing University
Nanjing Institute of Technology
Nankai University, Tianjin
Qinghua University, Beijing
Shandong University, Jinan
Shanghai Communications (Jiaotong) University
Sichuan University, Chengdu
South China (Huanan) Institute of Technology, Guangzhou
Tianjin University
Wuhan University
Xi'an Communications (Jiaotong) University
Xiamen University
Zhejiang University, Hangzhou
Zhongshan University, Guangzhou

My interviews also included two to three hours at each of eight secondary or "middle" schools—arranged by the universities wherever possible—primarily for the purpose of asking questions related to the college entrance examinations. My requests to visit ordinary (i.e., "non-keypoint") middle schools were never granted. All of the schools visited were among the best of the key middle schools in each city, with the exception of the technical school in Shanghai, which was also among the best of its kind and under the direct administration of the Number One Ministry of Machine Building in Beijing. Short interviews with a representative of the Shanghai Bureau of Higher Education (28 November) and the Education Ministry spokesman mentioned above (6 December) completed the research assignment. The middle schools visited were:

Chengdu Middle School Number Seven (15 May)

East China Teachers' Training University Number Two Affiliated Middle School, Shanghai (28 November)

Jinan Middle School Number Twenty-two (4 December)

Lanzhou Middle School Number Twenty-eight (8 May)

Nanjing Teachers' Training College Affiliated Middle School, formerly the Lu Xun Middle School (12 November)

Nankai Middle School, Tianjin (29 April)

Shanghai Machine Building School (19 November)

Xiamen Middle School Number Eight, now known by its pre-1965 name of Xiamen Double Ten Middle School (21 October)

Two of these middle schools, Nankai and the university-affiliated school in Shanghai, were among the twenty primary and secondary schools officially designated as national keypoints in January 1978. These, too, were originally supposed to be run directly by the Ministry of Education, but the ministry spokesman indicated that, like the full complement of national key universities, the ministry had found it impossible to administer directly so large a number of schools. The administration of all twenty of these key primary and middle schools had therefore been "sent down" or returned to the cities and provinces in which they are located.

I traveled alone, conducting and transcribing the interviews myself. Three universities provided English teachers to assist with translation; several others provided a speaker of clear *putonghua* to help mediate heavy local accents; and in some cases I was on my own. With the exception of course lists which were sometimes provided, all of the information was conveyed verbally.

Neither the CSCPRC nor the Chinese Ministry of Education should be held responsible for any of the information contained herein since neither participated in the preparation of the questionnaire nor in my interpretations of the answers given. Because of the general reluctance in China to speak to foreigners for attribution, I have refrained from identifying individuals, and sometimes their institutions as well, where the subject matter is especially sensitive. This seems especially necessary since this study focuses on some of the more controversial issues in Chinese higher education at present and my interpretation of them is often at variance with that of the administators I interviewed. It is even more frequently at variance with the official view as expressed by the Ministry of Education.

Considering the unusual nature of this project and the circumstances surrounding it, I was impressed by the candor and good humor which many administrators brought to the interviews. Some possessed these qualities to an outstanding degree, and I am especially grateful to those among them who accepted this exercise at face value, granting it neither more nor less importance than it deserved. A group of university administrators from the United States whose paths crossed mine at Wuhan helped place my work in sharper perspective. Taking one look at the questionnaire, they declared that if anyone presented such a list of questions to them they would most certainly show that person the door. By this standard my Chinese hosts responded well above and beyond the call of duty.

I am also grateful for the assistance provided by Liu Zicheng and Jean Xiong at the Universities Service Centre in Hong Kong. Their help was invaluable both in preparing for the interviews beforehand and in interpreting their contents afterward. Mr. Liu prepared a written Chinese translation of the questionnaire, and Ms. Xiong was responsible for clipping and filing a selection of local Chinese newspaper articles which made it possible to corroborate much of the information collected during the interviews.

As part of a larger research project on Chinese education, I have also been interviewing emigré teachers from China in Hong Kong. This interview material has not been used in the preparation of this report except in a few instances where information from the former had a direct bearing on the substance of the latter. These instances are identified in the text.

Finally, a note on terminology is perhaps necessary. The extent, nature, and duration of the Cultural Revolution is a subject of varying interpretation both among those who lived through it and those who have studied it. Some use the term only with reference to the 1966-68 period dominated by the radicalism of the Red Guard movement, which was curbed after the call to "return to school to make revolution." For them, everything after that call began to be implemented in 1968 and the Red Guards were mustered out of their schools to make way for the new students is referred to as "after the Cultural Revolution." For others, the cut-off date is the Ninth Communist Party Congress in 1969. Some cite the fall of Lin Biao two years later. Still others, attentive to the power and policy struggles of the 1970s, continued to refer then—and still do—to the entire period up to Mao's death in 1976 as the Cultural Revolution. This was the interpretation used by university administrators throughout my interviews and is the one that is followed in this monograph. In this interpretation, the Cultural Revolution is seen as a mass movement like several others that bear the Maoist imprint. It assumes that the excesses of the initial mass mobilization were instigated as a deliberate phase in order, among other things, to intimidate and control the existing powerholders. Once that was accomplished, a new and different order was supposed to be established at the hands of a new or at least reformed set of leaders. Thus the changes in education between 1968-76 are seen as a part of the entire process since they could not have been instituted under the pre-1966 leadership. The abrupt and comprehensive return to the pre-1966 forms and structures that occurred throughout the education system after 1976, and indeed in many other sectors as well, provides added justification for this interpretation.

INTRODUCTION

In a fascinating historical parallel with the imperial examinations of old, post-1949 China has elevated its national college entrance examinations to a position of far greater significance than such procedures usually enjoy in most countries. Among the first measures heralding the onset of the Cultural Revolution in 1966 was the suspension of these examinations. Similarly, at the end of the 1966-76 Cultural Revolution decade, following the death of Mao Zedong and the downfall of the "Gang of Four," this was among the first of the innovations associated with that decade to be overturned. The Eleventh National Congress of the Chinese Communist Party ceremoniously proclaimed the end of the Cultural Revolution in August 1977. The restoration of the college entrance examinations was officially announced two months later on 21 October.[1]

Their shifting political fortunes indicate the regard in which the examinations are held. They are seen as more than the guardians of the gateway to life's most valued aims. The privileged minority who gain access to a higher education achieve a status in society not unlike the degree-holders of dynastic times. The examinations are therefore associated with the reproduction of a social elite. The values and interests of that elite have often been at variance with those of the post-1949 political leadership which has not been drawn from among the college-educated. Yet the examinations were also allowed to determine the structure and content of the larger education system in order to produce the talent required by a modernizing nation.

Because of their symbolic and practical significance, and the contradictions inherent therein, the college entrance examinations became a focal point for the "struggle between the two lines" in education. Throughout the 1966-76 decade when that struggle dominated all aspects of China's political life, the examinations were denounced as a key feature of the conventional education system that was perpetuating Chinese traditions of intellectual and social elitism. It was argued then that to use the examinations as the primary determinant of access to higher education restricted that opportunity to those with access to the best secondary schooling, which was in turn restricted to those with the best primary schooling. And this, as all teachers know, depends in large measure on who the parents are. It is a commonplace in Chinese educational circles that the children of educated people, or "intellectuals," generally perform better in school because their parents value learning, provide the necessary home environment, and make every effort to ensure that their children enroll in the best schools available. Certain assumptions of genetic superiority appear to underlie this cultural inheritance argument but are less frequently articulated.

In order to prevent the existing educated elite from reproducing itself in this manner, enrollment policies had been used, marginally in the 1950s and increasingly thereafter, to restrict the access of children from such families to a college education, regardless of academic merit. By the mid-1960s, those whose access was so restricted included youths from capitalist, landlord, and rich-peasant families, as well as those whose immediate family members had been convicted of committing serious errors, whether of a criminal or political nature, both before 1949 and after. The beneficiaries of these policies were young people from "good" family backgrounds, that is, from working-class families and the children of leading officials or cadres in good political standing.

These policies culminated in the Cultural Revolution, which abolished the national entrance examinations altogether and changed the rules governing access to higher education. Beginning around 1970 as institutions of higher learning reopened, all young people with a few exceptions were required to work for at least two years before entering college. The work requirement officially transformed the young people into "workers, peasants, and soldiers" whatever their family origin, although the new status was not strong enough to override the old biases against potential college candidates with problematic family backgrounds.

During the 1970-76 period, the nomination of college candidates was determined largely but not solely by the leaders of the applicants' work units. A fixed number of places in college, specified by school and major in accordance with an overall enrollment plan, was assigned directly to individual communes and factories or work units. Following a process of recommendation and nomination within the work unit itself, each unit's top leaders enjoyed the final right of decision as to which of its young people were designated to fill the assigned college places. A "cultural assessment" was usually one of several criteria used in helping arrive at this decision, together with the applicant's work record and family history. But academic achievement was reduced to secondary importance at best.

The final selection was usually left to the university enrollment inspectors who journeyed around the country every year. Each school was responsible for sending its representatives to the localities where it had been assigned admissions quotas in accordance with the predetermined plan. These representatives sometimes interviewed the candidates and sometimes relied on a perusal of their files only. Usually, the number of candidates nominated was slightly larger than the number of college places available, allowing the enrollment officers a limited margin for choice. The children and relations of cadres or office-holders—local as well as leading, and rural as well as urban—appear to have been been the major beneficiaries of this enrollment system. This is because it was open to influence-peddling and parental pressure at all levels given the pivotal role of local leaders in the nominating process.

Since preparing students to pass the college entrance exams was thus eliminated as the *raison d'être* of secondary schooling, the entire system could be restructured in accordance with the egalitarian ideals that dominated official rhetoric during the 1966-76 decade. Mass education was expanded at the primary and secondary levels, while elite education was drastically disrupted and curtailed. The keypoint school system was abolished. This had channeled the best students as determined by their scores on the secondary school entrance exams into the best or college preparatory schools. Everyone was supposed to attend school in their own neighborhoods. Streaming of students by ability was forbidden as were a host of other practices that had grown up around the "examination life" that dominated the old school system. All the features of that system that had contributed toward the production of an educated elite were criticized and dismantled. The new system that was to have replaced the old was aimed at training a different kind of working-class intellectual.

The radical effort to remodel the old education system came to an abrupt halt after 1976 when the new post-Mao Government came to power. All the innovations of the Cultural Revolution decade were then themselves dismantled. The college entrance examinations were restored, the work requirement prior to college dropped, and strictures against the offspring of traditional elites lifted fully for the first time in three decades. The declared achievement is to have restored academic excellence to its rightful place as the chief criterion governing access to a higher education.

It would require more extensive research than is likely to be possible in China for many years hence to convince either detractors or supporters of this system that the college entrance examinations in particular do not merit the central role they have been given in the educational process. In the meantime, the restoration of the examinations at the apex of the school system and as the centerpiece of the post-Cultural Revolution enrollment process symbolizes the victory of the anti-Mao forces that dominate the present Government. Despite ongoing internal controversy, therefore, the examinations are likely to be maintained as much for the political motivations inherent in that victory as for the academic purpose they serve.

Within this political context and the pro-examination, anti-Cultural Revolution bias which colors all official discourse at present, the university administrators interviewed for this study were willing to describe and discuss present enrollment policies and practices in considerable detail. Some of the information they provided is not available elsewhere; some elaborated upon cursory commentaries published in newspapers and journals; and some only hinted at developing trends and internal disputes. What follows here is primarily a presentation of the information collected during these interviews, integrated and augmented wherever possible with contemporary published accounts. Reflecting the larger social and academic significance of college enrollment in China, the body of data provides insights and raises questions on a range of issues that extend well beyond the relatively simple task of admitting students to college. The data also reveal some of the main areas which fueled the fires of disagreement between the Cultural Revolution "line" on education policy and that being promoted by the current leadership. Despite the official façade of unity, these points remain sources of continuing controversy today.

With the abandonment of the entire Cultural Revolution experiment, which aimed at equalizing the quality and quantity of education available to different sectors of the population, the college entrance examinations have been allowed to resume their dominant role within the education system. Among the most far-reaching consequences of this decision is its impact on the structures and forms of secondary education. The expansion and strengthening of the secondary school curriculum is only one of the consequences. Others entail major cutbacks in senior secondary enrollments and the closure of senior secondary schools throughout the country. The announced plan for those remaining involves the creation of two clear streams: college preparatory on the one hand and vocational on the other. These decisions are being rationalized everywhere, in both city and countryside, as necessary to enhance the quality of education. In the process, resources both human and material are being reconcentrated in the college preparatory, or keypoint schools.

Within the college preparatory stream, passing the college entrance examinations has once again become the chief reason for existence and the object of everyone's efforts. Cramming and competition to boost pass rates are routinely criticized and the criticism routinely ignored. The logic of the system dictates that result since its structures and functions have all been redrawn to reward the single aim of producing successful college candidates. Fujian province's remarkable performance on the 1978 and 1979 examinations has been traced directly to that province's methods of preparing its candidates for the entrance examinations. In tacit acknowledgment of the general disapproval such methods inspire, the lessons of Fujian's success were not advertised. But the whole nation has long since hastened to learn the jealously guarded secrets of that province's success, and universities continue to welcome its students because of the high scores they obtain on the college entrance examinations.

High scores alone are not enough to ensure admission to college, however. Politics and family background can still prevent an otherwise qualified candidate from gaining admission to college, although the relevant problems that can have this result have been redefined and significantly reduced. Virtually all of the categories of political and social problems that have served as the basis of reverse discrimination in college admission at various times since the 1950s have now been eliminated.

Meanwhile, health qualifications are rigorous and will become even more so if plans announced in 1981 to enforce the national physical fitness standards as a prerequisite for college admission are ever implemented. The physical and sexual stereotypes now reflected in China's college admissions policies would be viewed as an anachronistic holdover from a bygone era if discovered on some isolated provincial campus. That they are currently being promoted by the Ministries of Education and Health impels us to ask whether this can actually be the same society which less than a decade ago proclaimed that "women hold up half the universe."

Equally surprising, if one were to have taken at face value the previous uniform declarations to place the national interest above all other considerations, are the current preferences of college candidates as revealed on their application forms. Everyone agrees that the desire for a safe, secure, and comfortable future is now the dominant concern. College administrators in their forties and fifties recall the enthusiasm which inspired many of their generation to work for the New China during the decade after 1949. There is, they acknowledge, no comparable idealism among the current college-age population.

At the same time, the game-plan approach to the individual's preference has been restored in full. The candidates' listed preferences must be based on a calculation of the schools and specialties to which they have the most realistic chance of being admitted. An inappropriate listing of preferences can result in failure to be admitted to any school, despite an otherwise satisfactory record of achievement. Academic objectives and career choices must be carefully balanced against this calculation when the application forms are written.

During the first years after the restoration of the national college entrance examinations, however, their administration at least appeared less open to behind-the-scenes abuse than at any earlier period. This is because the minimum passing scores were publicly announced, each candidate was notified of his/her individual score, and all had the right to request a review of the correction process in case of doubt. But by the early 1980s, the system was moving inexorably back toward its pre-1966 format, as the minimum passing scores were gradually withdrawn from public view and the right to request a review was abolished.

Additional changes were introduced in 1980-81, which will allow the universities more latitude, both officially and otherwise, to manipulate the selection process to their own advantage. One such change gives the individual key universities the right to pass over up to 20 percent of their quotas in any given province if the scores there do not meet the university's own standards. The key universities are also permitted to establish special links with the best key secondary schools in their vicinity and to give preference in admission to their graduates. These measures have been granted at the demand of the key universities in order to guarantee further the quality of their student bodies. In the process, they have restored to these secondary schools the privileged status they enjoyed before the Cultural Revolution.

At the same time, the dossier or file system is being reestablished. Under this system, academic, health, and political/deportment records for each semester of senior secondary school are to be submitted for reference as part of the college enrollment procedure. The inspiration for this change appears to have come from two very different sources. On the one hand, the Ministry of Education is aware of foreign, or at least American, criticism to the effect that a single examination score is not an adequate measure of intellectual ability. This seems to have inspired the move to begin using secondary school academic records "for reference." On the other hand, there is also internal political criticism within China over the importance attached to academic achievement as the sole criterion for admission to college. New requirements introduced in 1980 and 1981 require the university not only to use the candidates' secondary school records for reference but to grant a certain degree of preference to the political activists among them.

Whether this last requirement can actually be enforced, given the concurrent measures which grant the key universities greater autonomy in enrollment for the purpose of enhancing the scholastic quality of their student bodies, remains an open question. The substantive nature of the added political criterion also remains open to question, since academic achievement appears to have become the principal condition for student membership in the Communist Youth League as well as in naming "three-goods" students—two formal indicators of political activism.

The key universities are, moreover, required to make few concessions to the disadvantaged sectors of Chinese society. These schools were in 1980 subject to no fixed quotas for any category of student. Nor were students from working-class backgrounds, officially favored in the past, granted any form of preference on grounds of class origin in any kind of college or university. The problem of the educationally disadvantaged is now treated primarily as one of regional imbalance in the development of education, rather than as a function of the social inequalities between the existing college-educated elite and the working class or between town and countryside. The problem is therefore being addressed primarily through the provincial balance built into the annual unified enrollment plans. And within each provincial enrollment quota, the major responsibility for accommodating the disadvantaged areas lies with the ordinary provincial institutions of higher learning and primarily with the junior colleges among them. The key universities would admit to relaxing their admissions standards only in rare circumstances.

The current reluctance to release statistics on the social composition of the college population is undoubtedly related to the internal controversy created by these fundamental changes in the rules governing access to a college education. Yet to be identified and measured, therefore, are the social and political consequences of removing the constraints not only *against* the traditional elites but also *in favor of* those sectors of the population that have heretofore constituted the main official beneficiaries of Communist rule.

The Unified Enrollment Plan

Freshman enrollment takes place each year on the basis of a national unified plan drawn up by the Ministry of Education in conjunction with the National Planning Commission. The size of each province's total annual enrollment quota is now roughly the same from one year to the next. It is fixed essentially on the basis of two considerations, corresponding roughly to supply and demand. The supply side reflects a province's educational development as measured by the number of its graduating middle school seniors; the province's past performance on the college entrance exams; and the number of colleges it has, since a majority of students are assigned to schools within their home province. According to these criteria, the more educationally developed a province, the larger its annual freshman enrollment quotes.

Balanced against these considerations, however, is each province's demand or need for college graduates. Thus the provincial enrollment quotas that would emerge solely on the basis of proportional educational development are moderated to a certain extent by considerations of relative deprivation. Hence Zhejiang, a high-scoring educationally developed province, has somewhat smaller annual enrollment quotas than it might otherwise be entitled to, while those of the more backward Gansu are somewhat larger. But the precise formula whereby these considerations are balanced to make up the final calculation of each province's yearly enrollment plan was not revealed.

It should be pointed out that the provincial enrollment quota is not the number of students to be enrolled in that province's institutions of higher learning each year but rather the total number of its own native sons and daughters to be enrolled both within the home province and outside of it. Thus, of more than 17,000 new students enrolled in Beijing's institutions of higher learning in 1979, only some 7,700 were from Beijing. Beijing's own enrollment quota that year was actually 11,000, of which some 3,000 students were assigned to schools in outlying provinces.[2] Selected provincial quotas gleaned from the press and interview data are shown in table 1 (pp. 123-25).

With the total provincial quotas thus roughly set and similar in size from one year to the next, the universities nevertheless play an important role in determining their own individual enrollment plans each year. The school calendar begins on 1 September or shortly thereafter. The preparation of the enrollment plan for the key universities begins approximately one year in advance of this date, when the Education Ministry circulates among them a document containing, among other data, two sets of figures. One set shows the number of graduating middle school seniors in every province; the other lists each province's scores on the college entrance examinations each year since they were restored in 1977. On the basis of these two sets of statistics, each university draws up its enrollment plan for the following academic year.

The university prepares its plan in detail, indicating not only the total number of students it wants to enroll, but the number to be enrolled in each major and/or academic department and the province from which each student in each major is to be recruited as well. Thus Nanjing University will specify the number of students in physics that it wants to enroll from Zhejiang province, the number in foreign languages from Shanghai, and so on. The plan is then sent up by the university in the form of a recommendation to the Ministry.[3]

Traditional patterns of achievement have reappeared since 1977, with the coastal provinces and autonomous cities (Beijing, Tianjin, and Shanghai) generally scoring higher than the inland areas. As a rule, therefore, the best of the key universities—Beijing, Qinghua, Chinese Science and Technology, and Fudan —are allowed to plan for more students from the high-scoring areas than are other schools. Moreover, in fixing their enrollment plans, the universities also consider certain divisions of labor associated with different regions and their particular needs and traditions. For example, students from the coastal provinces, and particularly the main coastal cities, are thought to have a greater aptitude for learning foreign languages and knowing how to deal with foreigners due to the long exposure of those areas to the outside world. This tradition is reflected in the university enrollment plans which allow for larger numbers of foreign-language majors from those areas than from the hinterland.

Similarly, students from the rural areas and county towns are said to score generally lower on the examinations than those from the major urban areas. Hence relatively more students from less urbanized provinces are planned for the less popular and/or "softer" subjects, where the lack of competition tends to depress admissions scores. These subjects include agronomy, forestry, biology, geology, geography, teacher training, Chinese language, history, and politics. "Urban" subjects are those such as physics, chemistry, computer science, and radio electronics, which are the most popular and therefore have the highest admissions standards. Big-city students tend to monopolize these subjects because of their generally higher performance on the examinations, and the universities build this consideration, too, into their enrollment plans.

In addition, a certain major, or specialty *(zhuanye)*, to use the Chinese term, may be taught in accordance with the needs of a particular region and enrollment quotas will therefore be concentrated in that area. In such cases, it is understood that the students will probably return there after graduation, and this consideration is built into the job-assignment plans for college graduates as well.

Finally, Ministry of Education regulations require the key universities and those non-key schools—of which there are many—that enroll outside their home provinces to concentrate enrollments regionally to the greatest extent possible. This is seen as the most rational means of accommodating communications problems and regional differences, most notably those of climate and diet. Universities located in the northern part of the country "face north" and enroll the majority, though not all, of their students from the northern provinces, while the same is true for southern schools. Greater numbers of students are always enrolled from the home province and those nearby, rather than from more distant locales.

Nankai University, for example, was required to enroll about one-third of its students from the city of Tianjin itself and another third from the North and Northeast, leaving only one-third to be enrolled from more distant provinces. Fudan University was enrolling 60-70 percent of its students from the Shanghai municipality. Jilin University's 1980 enrollment plan called for 62 percent from the home province and 38 percent from outside (mainly from Shanghai and Fujian). About two-thirds of Shandong University's student body was being recruited in the home province, while the remainder came from north, east, and northeast China. In 1977 students were drawn from as far away as Xinjiang, but this was found inappropriate, and the field has since been narrowed in what appears to be a general pattern for all the key universities.[4]

The Education Ministry decides whether or not to accept the preliminary enrollment plan devised by the individual university on the basis of these considerations. The tendency is for the universities to try to maximize the number of students to be enrolled from the high-scoring provinces while minimizing the overall enrollment figure. The role of the ministry, by contrast, is to ensure greater regional balance and to maximize the overall enrollment figure. Despite this difference in perspective, the changes introduced by the Ministry in a university's proposed enrollment plan are usually not great and are never made without prior consultation with the school concerned. East China Teachers' Training University, for instance, recommended a figure of 1,200 new students for 1980. The ministry countered with a larger figure, but the university held its ground and in the end enrolled only 1,241 students that year.

At Wuhan University, the university recommended a quota of 1,175 freshmen for 1980, a figure initially approved by the ministry but subsequently revised upwards after a new specialty, Scientific French, was added to the curriculum. This new major had a planned enrollment of only 20 students for its first year, 1980. The university actually enrolled a total of 1,214 new students that year, in accordance with a ruling that permits universities to exceed their enrollment plans by from 1 to 3 percent in anticipation of the inevitable few who drop out or are obliged to withdraw.

Extra-quota students, when admitted, are negotiated separately between the individual school and the locality or work unit sponsoring and financing them. Hence, Wuhan University agreed to enroll an additional 240 students in 1980, assigned by Hubei province to attend as commuters rather than regular students. Such students are being enrolled outside the national enrollment plan. When they graduate, the localities from which they originate will be responsible for employing them outside the national job-assignment plan for college graduates. The localities are also responsible for financing the schooling of such students outside the planned state budget for the university they attend. Expanded enrollment will be discussed in greater detail below.

Non-key universities arrange their individual enrollment quotas in the same manner, albeit with the provincial education bureaus rather than with the center directly. Overall quota figures for such schools are negotiated between the provinces and the center, with each province then dividing up the intra-provincial quota among its own schools. The comprehensive national plan, which is finalized by March or April for the coming academic year, comprises (1) the number of students to be enrolled under the plan in every institution of higher learning in the country; (2) the specialty or academic department in which each student will be enrolled; and (3) the province from which each student is to be recruited for each specialty or department. This full national enrollment plan is printed and circulated in book form to every college and university, but it is not issued to the general public. It is left to the individual provinces to decide how much of this information to publicize and in what manner to do so.

A survey of local newspapers available in 1981 indicated that only Zhejiang published in its provincial daily all of the data having to do with its own enrollment plan. This included the number of its students who would be admitted in each major or department at every school in the country enrolling Zhejiang students that year. For example, Sichuan University, the first listed, was scheduled to enroll a total of fifteen freshmen from Zhejiang, three in each of five majors: Chinese language, history, philosophy, physics, and chemistry.[5] As will be indicated below, considerable problems have been known to arise in provinces which do not fully publicize this information—as most apparently do not—for the candidates who must fill out their application forms without it.

General Eligibility

Since 1977, eligibility requirements to sit for the examinations have gradually narrowed the field of prospective candidates. The work requirement prior to college introduced during the Cultural Revolution decade has been dropped, and students are now selected primarily from a homogeneous pool of young senior middle school graduates.

According to the official enrollment regulations, applicants must have graduated from senior middle school or be at an equivalent educational level. They must also be unmarried, in good health, and under twenty-five years of age. The maximum age was extended up to thirty in 1977 and 1978 to give members of the "Cultural Revolution generation" a chance to recoup opportunities lost during that decade. In 1979 the maximum age was reduced to twenty-eight, and enrollment of students over twenty-five discouraged. The maximum age limit was reduced to twenty-five in 1982.

It was also announced in 1979 that henceforth those already employed, whether blue- or white-collar workers, should seek to improve their cultural level primarily through spare-time education and not as regular college students. Such people in both state and collective enterprises must first obtain the permission of their work units to sit for the college entrance exams.[6]

Those defined as ineligible to take the examinations include individuals currently enrolled in a number of different education programs for working people; graduates of specialized technical secondary schools who have not worked for at least two years following graduation; students still studying in secondary school; and those who were accepted the previous year by an institution of higher learning to which they had applied but who refused to accept assignment there. Persons in this latter category are, however, permitted to sit for the examinations again the second year after refusing such an assignment. Candidates may otherwise take the examinations an unlimited number of times until they reach the maximum age limit but, according to some administrators, most give up after the third unsuccessful attempt.[7]

The increasingly strict requirements have produced a steady decline in the number of candidates sitting for the examination each year (see table 2, p. 125). This is in line with official policy, which is now deliberately striving to reduce the number of candidates through a variety of other means as well. The most effective of these are naturally the preliminary, or qualifying, examinations *(yukao)*. A number of provinces had been experimenting with such preliminary examinations since 1977, although the practice seems not to have been actively promoted until 1980-81. In 1980, seven provinces gave such exams. The number rose to thirteen in 1981, and the practice is to be extended to all provinces as local conditions permit.

In 1981, the senior secondary school graduation examinations most commonly doubled as the qualifying exam. "Eligibility" to take the national unified examinations, i.e., the number of those allowed to pass the preliminaries, is relative to each province's university enrollment quota. The ratios used by the provinces to determine that eligibility vary between 3:1 and 5:1. In the thirteen provinces giving such preliminary exams in 1981, the pool of applicants was reduced from 3,680,000 to 1,260,000.[8]

Officially, the smaller number of candidates is said to enhance efficiency by allowing the national examinations to be given at only one site in each county. Correction work can then be similarly concentrated and unified within each province. And college teachers can take over the entire task without having to rely on those from the secondary level, as was being done in the late 1970s.

Less officially, university administrators acknowledged that the preliminary examinations were being promoted in order to reduce the large investment of money and manpower necessary to administer the national examinations to millions of candidates each year, the great majority of whom must fail in any case. But administrators also noted that the preliminary exams were not uniformly welcomed by local educators, who were now responsible for administering not one but two sets of examinations.

CHAPTER I

Preparation:
Restructuring Secondary Education

The use of the middle school graduation examinations as a qualifying criterion for the national college entrance exams highlights the crucial role that college enrollment once again plays as the culmination of a student's secondary school career. Indeed, the entire school system now appears to have been restructured with the primary aim of nurturing talent *(peiyang rencai)* for college, that is, preparing and selecting the approximately 300,000 students who will enter institutions of higher learning each year. The reversal of the Cultural Revolution decade's emphasis on expanding general secondary education has been rationalized in terms of the very limited numbers that can be accommodated in college, as though that were the chief aim of such schooling.

When the policy change was announced in 1979, it was pointed out that the number of students then graduating from secondary schools each year—7.2 million at that time—was far greater than the annual enrollment of the nation's colleges could ever be in the foreseeable future. Moreover, the rapid development of secondary schooling during the Cultural Revolution decade was said to have "spread financial resources very thinly and aggravated the shortage of qualified teachers."[1]

The answer, as dictated by the post-Mao strategy of educational development, is to reduce drastically secondary school enrollment, close large numbers of middle schools, and reorient those remaining in the direction of technical and vocational training. Thus not only are Cultural Revolution policies now said to have tried to universalize *(puji)* secondary schooling prematurely, but it is also claimed that they sought to unify *(danyihua)* education in a manner inappropriate to China's needs and level of economic development. The new policies now being implemented seek to reverse the "equalization" of both the quantity and quality of education that occurred as a result of Cultural Revolution educational policies.

Cutting Back at the Secondary Level

In 1977 there were 584,000 students in China's colleges and universities. By the 1980-81 academic year, the figure was just over 1 million.[2] During that same time, however, the number of students at the secondary level was reduced by close to 14 million. These official statistics highlight the key difference between the now discredited strategy of educational development promoted during the Cultural Revolution years and the one currently being implemented. The increasing number of college students by comparison with the 1966-76 decade is among the most highly publicized features of present education policies, together with the new emphasis on quality and the increased receptivity to Western influence. Much less visible are the costs of implementing these policies and the social assumptions on which they are based.

In 1965 the total number of students in China's secondary schools was 14.4 million, as shown in table 3 (p. 126). The figure for the 1977-78 academic year was 68.9 million, with an additional million enrolled in various kinds of specialized schools. The new policies commenced with the 1978-79 academic year. The State Statistical Bureau acknowledged in its reports a decline in national secondary school enrollments totaling 10 million for the two years 1979 and 1980. By comparison with the earlier 68.9 million enrollment figure for 1977-78, however, the 55 million announced by the bureau for 1980 indicated a decline of nearly 14 million. During 1980 alone, also according to official statistics, the new policy resulted in the closure of 23,700 secondary schools.[3]

The cutbacks have been most severe at the senior secondary level where, according to a claim made in the *Guangming ribao* of 12 October 1981, enrollments for the 1981-82 academic year were down by approximately two-thirds as compared with 1978. The reductions that occurred that year, mentioned below with specific reference to Shanghai and Beijing, are not reflected in table 3, which covers the 1980-81 academic year.

Nor has the increase in technical and vocational school enrollments been sufficient to match this reduction in general secondary schooling, as can also be seen from table 3. Indeed, there has been no hint of any attempt at an immediate proportional shift of student bodies from general to technical schools. The decision to curtail the former is being implemented separately throughout the country, in rural areas as well as in the largest cities.

Although there is an awareness of the relationship between demography and educational development, there is no evidence of any effort to coordinate the reduction of secondary school enrollments with the declining numbers of that age group. The primary and even secondary school populations are already declining in some cities, most notably Shanghai, where birth control began to be seriously promoted in the early 1970s and even earlier by some accounts. But the curtailment of secondary schooling has been immediate and has proceeded independently of this demographic trend, as well as of the expansion of technical and vocational secondary schooling.

General "internal" guidelines for the cutback were issued in 1978 and, according to hearsay evidence, were similar in a number of different provinces. The proportion of those not allowed to pass the entrance exams into junior middle school was not to exceed around 20 percent province-wide, while the proportion not allowed to pass into senior middle school was not to exceed 40 percent. Those initial guidelines were apparently phrased in such a way as to leave considerable leeway in local implementation.

According to a schoolteacher from Hainan Island interviewed in Hong Kong, the prefectural city of Haikou simply refused to reduce enrollments the first year after the guidelines were issued on grounds that it would create too many unemployed. By 1981, however, only 70 percent of the primary school graduates in the provincial capital, Guangzhou, who took the entrance exams for junior middle school were admitted. The remaining 30 percent were permitted to repeat the final year of primary school in preparation for a second try at the entrance exams. Guangzhou's pass rate for senior middle school in 1981 was 75 percent of those taking the entrance exams.[4] The city of Guangzhou had previously boasted universal ten-year schooling (five years of primary and five years of secondary).

School administrators in Xiamen (Amoy) and Nanjing claimed that about 80 percent of those taking the entrance exams in their cities were accepted into senior middle school as of 1980. The city of Fuzhou in 1981 announced that within the city proper, 91 percent of those taking the entrance exams for junior middle school were enrolled; the average pass rate for city and suburbs combined was only 81 percent. At the senior secondary level, the pass rate for Fuzhou alone was 73.6 percent, while the city-suburb average stood at 65 percent.[5]

By contrast, Shandong's provincial capital, Jinan, was like Haikou in resisting the trend. The reason, it was said, was to retain universal schooling at least through the junior level. Students in Jinan who failed the city-wide entrance examinations to junior middle school were being assigned to their nearest neighborhood schools "because we cannot just send such youngsters out onto the streets." They were being placed in slow streams and taught according to a locally devised syllabus rather than the national unified teaching plan, which is geared to the level of the keypoint schools.[6]

Elsewhere, however, the cutbacks have been far more drastic. Statistics now available for Beijing, Shanghai, Liaoning, and Jiangsu all show reductions at the senior secondary level far in excess of the earlier guidelines. The two cities had only just in recent years achieved universal ten-year schooling.

Initial reductions in Shanghai had been marginal. Administrators there claimed that 85-90 percent of the age group was studying in senior middle school as of 1980. But they told of plans for a major reduction in the number of senior middle schools, scheduled to go into effect in Shanghai at the start of the 1981-82 academic year, which would significantly reduce that percentage. And, in fact, of the 75,000 junior middle graduates in the entire Shanghai municipality in 1981, only slightly more than 20,000, or 30 percent at most, were allowed to pass the entrance exams and continue on to the senior secondary level.[7]

Despite Shanghai's larger total population, the earlier attention paid to birth control there has resulted in a significantly smaller secondary school age cohort than is the case in Beijing. Until the 1981-82 academic year, reductions in the latter city's senior secondary enrollments were reportedly confined largely to the suburban areas. These reductions are shown in the following tabulation of Beijing's senior secondary enrollment figures from 1965 through 1980:[8]

Year	Number of Schools	Number of Students
1965	122	53,000 (three-year system)
1977	1,072	457,000 (two-year system)
1980	—	317,000 (two-year system)

In 1981, however, only 54,000, or 39 percent of Beijing's total 139,000 junior secondary graduates, were admitted to the senior middle level.[9]

According to the Beijing regulations—and those for Guangzhou as well—junior middle graduates not passing the entrance exams to the next level can attend special make-up classes organized by their schools or neighborhoods for one year to prepare for a second try at the exams. Those who fail a second time must leave school to "await employment."[10] According to a well-informed interviewee from Guangzhou, however, that city's senior secondary enrollments remained essentially unchanged in 1982 from the 1981 level cited above. The issue of reducing them to the new lows achieved by Shanghai and Beijing resulted in an intense debate among municipal education bureau leaders who decided temporarily against the more drastic reduction.

In Jiangsu province, it was reported in 1980 that 80 percent of those graduating from primary school go on to junior middle school (about 95 percent in the cities); but only 30 percent of all those graduating from junior secondary schools are now going on to the senior level (about 60 percent in the cities). Between 1976 and 1979, annual province-wide enrollment in senior middle schools dropped from 500,000 to 270,000, and official plans aimed to retain that level of enrollment for some years to come. The successful effects of the province's birth control program were only just beginning to be registered in a decline in the primary school population.[11]

In Liaoning province, the number of middle schools was reduced between 1978 and 1980, from 3,000-plus to about 600. In accordance with a preannounced plan, commune senior middle schools are being abolished, leaving only a few senior secondary schools in each county. Also being abolished are junior middle classes attached to the primary schools run by production brigades within communes, one means widely used in the countryside to boost secondary school enrollments there during the Cultural Revolution decade. The rule is that henceforth each commune will run only one junior middle school. Between 1978 and 1981, 3,000 of the total 7,111 such attached junior middle classes were abolished, and the remainder were awaiting the same fate. The total senior secondary enrollments in the province had grown to 1,423,000 in 1977, or eighteen times the 1965 figure. By 1980 there were only 140,000 students in general senior secondary schools, with an additional 171,000 enrolled in a variety of technical and vocational schools.[12]

The Liaoning cutbacks appear extreme. Foreign visitors to other provinces have been told of reductions there more comparable to those in Jiangsu. In 1980, the head of a county education bureau in yet another province acknowledged in a conversation with me that about two-thirds of the communes in his county had established their own senior middle schools by the end of the Cultural Revolution decade. By 1980, however, half of these schools had already been closed, "because their quality was so low." Foreign visitors have also learned of similar commune senior middle school closures in the suburbs of Shanghai.

These deliberate cutbacks in accordance with state policy have occurred simultaneously with the now officially acknowledged rising attrition rates in the rural areas, a result of the new agricultural policies.[13] The incentives to participate in the individual family's money-making endeavors are now greater than ever before, outweighing in many a rural household's calculation the benefits to be obtained from educating its children.[14]

In a mutually reinforcing interaction, moreover, these individual family decisions parallel the new emphasis on reducing the expenditures of the collective in deference to expanding individual peasant incomes. Unfortunately for rural education, it falls in the category of collective expenditure, which has meant reductions in production-brigade financing for local schools. Previously, pressure from above forced the brigades to allocate fixed proportions of their collective incomes to finance their own schools. Now the collectives have much more freedom in deciding how to allocate their incomes, which are in any case declining due to the transfer of collectively run endeavors to individual peasants. This has created an added economic incentive for closing and/or consolidating primary as well as junior middle schools and classes at the brigade level.

Finally, this trend is being encouraged by the educational authorities themselves, who have admitted privately to foreigners, if not yet for domestic publication, that peasant boys learn most of what they need to know about tilling the land from their fathers. That being the case, local education bureaus are no longer promoting the expansion of education in rural areas where the level of agricultural technology does not require it.

The net result of these changing policies and the official assumptions underlying them is a declining percentage of the age group claimed to be entering primary school: that is, from "over 95 percent" in 1977 to 93 percent in 1981. Of the latter percentage, only about 60 percent are thought to finish primary school.[15]

No current national estimates of pass rates from the primary to the junior middle levels are available. Vice-Premier Chen Muhua's frequently cited estimate of 88 percent was made in mid-1979, when the reductions had just begun.[16] According to population estimates provided in a new theoretical publication, *Journal of the Dialectics of Nature*, there were in 1980 approximately 150 million young people in China between twelve and seventeen years of age. Hence only about 36 percent of that age group were in middle school at that time, according to the official 55 million secondary school enrollment figure.[17] Finally, according to estimates based on urban statistics only, at most about 40 percent of those graduating from junior middle school were by 1981 continuing on to the senior level.[18]

China is, it should be noted, in the process of converting back to the pre-1966 twelve-year school system, that is, six years of primary and six years of secondary, with the latter divided into three years each at the junior and senior levels. This is necessary, it is argued, because the newly unified national primary and secondary school curriculum, which is geared to the level of the key schools, creates too much pressure on the students when taught within a nine- or ten-year syllabus. Some provinces had established four-year secondary school systems during the Cultural Revolution decade while others had five-year systems.

Theoretically, therefore, the reduction in the number of students at the senior secondary level need not mark a significant decline in the amount of education available. *If* universal primary and junior secondary education were to be maintained, the majority would receive a total of nine years of schooling. That this is clearly not the case, however, is indicated by the increasing drop-out rates in the rural areas and the growing proportion not gaining admission at the junior secondary level.

Thus, the net result of the present strategy of educational development is to narrow and sharpen the pyramid: a few will receive much more education in terms of both quantity and quality, while more young people will actually be receiving less—although what they receive will presumably be of better quality than it was previously.

But while it is no longer fashionable in China to speak in terms of socialist ideals, the problems remain and so do the critics. "It is unthinkable to rely on such a composition of the population to build a modern nation," wrote the author of the above-cited study in *Dialectics of Nature*. Focusing on the quality over quantity bias of present education policies, he hypothesized as to the future of the 322 million young persons ranging in age from six to eighteen years given the existing level of educational development as of 1980. Some 20 million would grow up illiterate; at least 133 million would have no more than a primary school education; and only 10 million would receive any kind of professional secondary or tertiary level schooling. Arguing that quantity and quality were two sides of the same coin, he criticized the current one-sided emphasis on the latter. "We should correct this right now," he concluded, "rather than wait until future generations sum up lessons when they write history."

Professional and Vocational Secondary Schools

As for the qualitative equalization of education that occurred during the Cultural Revolution, much is now made of the ratios between general middle schools, on the one hand, and the specialized professional *(zhongdeng zhuanye xuexiao)* and vocational *(zhiye xuexiao)* schools on the other.[19] For example, this ratio was said to be 12:1 in Beijing and 5:1 in Tianjin in 1979, with similarly high ratios obtaining elsewhere. One province, Jiangsu, claimed its ratio to be 40:1. The pre-1966 ratio of approximately 1:1 was initially hailed as the most rational use of educational resources, since graduates of general schools are said to need two or three years of training to prepare them for the kinds of jobs in which the majority will be earning their living.[20]

As with the early guidelines announced for the cutbacks in secondary school enrollments, however, the reality of the plans for technical-vocational training now appear to be considerably in excess of the goals initially proclaimed. Indeed, the plan as of 1980-81 was to transform all remaining non-keypoint general middle schools into professional and/or vocational institutions at the senior level. This would finalize the division that has reemerged with the best or key schools having already become the main college preparatory stream. Administrators at one professional secondary school in Shanghai acknowledged that such a plan was being discussed but said that no final decision had yet been made. In their view, it would be a difficult plan to implement, given the capital expenditures and personnel changes necessary to convert ordinary schools to technical and professional facilities. As a "transitional" measure, some vocational courses are being introduced into the curriculum of general middle schools as conditions permit.[21]

In the much smaller city of Xiamen, the decision had already been made, as of 1980, to transform the senior sections of all non-keypoint, general secondary schools into vocational institutions. A few had already begun offering vocational courses, with one class of students studying accounting at one school and a class studying sewing at another. (In all Chinese schools at all levels, students are grouped into *ban*, or classes, all the members of which are taught together as a unit. Hence to introduce an accounting class means not that such a course is being offered but that one class of students has been formed to major in accounting.) The keypoint schools of Xiamen have not been given the task of teaching such courses, and the city's seven professional secondary *(zhongzhuan)* schools will remain unchanged in number. Additional vocational courses have since been set up, however, to train personnel for the new foreign investment zone being established on Xiamen Island. Suburban senior middle schools are supposed to be transformed into agricultural middle schools, although not all had begun this transformation by late 1980.[22]

Virtually identical plans were announced for Shandong province in 1981. One-third or more of the province's ordinary general senior middle schools in the cities are scheduled for conversion into vocational schools *(zhiye jishu zhongxue)*. As conditions permit, general middle schools in the countryside are to be converted to agricultural middle schools. Meanwhile, all remaining non-key general schools, whether urban or rural, are to introduce production-skills training *(shengchan jishu jiaoyu)*.[23]

These local plans are based on a "Report of the Ministry of Education and the National General Labor Bureau on the Restructuring of Secondary Education," approved by the State Council on 7 October 1980. According to this report, "a few ordinary senior middle schools are to be converted into vocational and agricultural middle schools," while the curriculum of all remaining ordinary senior middle schools is to be changed to include vocational subjects.[24]

Keypoint Schools

Equally significant are the changes that have occurred within the general secondary schools themselves in the process of re-creating the keypoint system with all its attendant tracks and streams. Key schools now exist at all levels, primary and secondary as well as tertiary.

The history of the keypoint school system appears lost in the mists of time. The question was asked at every university visited and most of the middle schools as well. But no one could give a definitive answer concerning the origin of the system or who was responsible for it. The Education Ministry spokesman gave the most detailed answer which was at least not contradicted elsewhere.

The ministry spokesman denied that the system had been inspired in any way by the Soviet Union, as were so many features of Chinese education introduced in the 1950s. Rather the system owes its origins to the keypoint concept that constituted the basis of the communists' economic development strategy during the anti-Japanese and civil wars of 1937-49. This strategy concentrated manpower and materiel for the purpose of economic construction in the impoverished border regions, which served as the base areas of the Chinese Communist movement.

The concept was subsequently applied to educational development as well. This step is traced to a now widely cited directive issued by Mao Zedong in 1953 to run keypoint middle schools well, although the directive was not publicized at that time. It was not until 1959, during the Great Leap Forward, that keypoint middle schools began to be established in a determined fashion. This followed Zhou Enlai's "Government Work Report" to a meeting of the People's Congress that year, in which he advocated the keypoint system for full-day schools at all levels: primary, secondary, and tertiary. Key schools were seen as the means to maintain quality within the context of the rapid expansion of mass education then underway.

Despite the existence of key schools from the mid-1950s on, then, the system was not developed on a nationwide scale until the 1960-66 period. Although the keypoint concept in economic development was retained, the Cultural Revolution attacked the elitist social consequences of its application in education. Since 1976, of course, the keypoint system has been revitalized at every level. Thus, the best teachers and administrators (as measured by seniority and educational level) and the best students (as measured by their entrance examination scores) are now being concentrated in the few best schools, both primary and secondary, in any given locality.

There have been widespread reports of entrance examinations for the key primary schools. But no amount of questioning could clarify how this examination method of enrollment is reconciled with the neighborhood-school principle still claimed to be in effect at the primary level. According to one press account from Tianjin, the key primary schools simply enroll the best children *(zeyou luqu)* from within the district boundaries drawn for each school.[25] Officially, the key primary schools are not supposed to give entrance exams, which accounts for the reluctance to answer this question. These exams are regarded as a clear indication of the unfair advantage that accrues to the offspring of educated parents. Only such children or those who have attended a good kindergarten would be able to recognize several hundred Chinese characters and solve the arithmetic problems that are said to be required to pass some of these examinations.

One key middle school principal, while denying that the key primary schools in that city gave entrance exams, nevertheless acknowledged that more of his students came from such schools than from the ordinary ones. But he insisted that the key primaries enroll only within their own neighborhoods. They are able to produce students who score higher on their secondary school entrance examinations for two reasons: (1) their teachers are better, and this alone is sufficient to produce higher examination scores from their students; and (2) the key primary school might be located in a neighborhood with many intellectual families, in which case its students would achieve higher scores because such children as a general rule outperform others.[26]

At the secondary level, there is now typically one keypoint middle school in each county and one or more in each city district, depending on population density and cultural level. Additional schools usually serve in a more comprehensive capacity as all-city keypoints; the highest-scoring students from the entire city are channeled into them.

As of late 1980, for example, there were a total of forty-eight district key middle schools in Shanghai's ten urban districts and twenty-five all-city keypoints. In the city of Jinan, four key schools enrolled on an all-city basis at both junior and senior levels, while five schools enrolled within individual city districts only. Lanzhou, however, had only five key middle schools, each serving one city district. A sixth district with a large concentration of factories had no key middle school, and students there were not permitted to attend schools in other districts. There were no key schools in Lanzhou enrolling on an all-city basis.[27]

The key schools are favored with larger budgets than others, the main difference being in the proportions allocated for building construction and the acquisition of equipment. One key school visited reported allocations of 50,000 *rmb* in 1978 and 30,000 *rmb* in 1979 for the purchase of new equipment. Ordinary schools in the same city were each granted only about 5,000 *rmb* annually for this same budgetary item. The key schools were also given such extras as television sets, tape recorders, and video-recording equipment, items outside their allocated equipment expenditures. Similarly, as part of the effort to upgrade the quality of keypoint schools in Shandong, provincial authorities there announced plans in early 1981 to divert to them 30-50 percent of the building construction funds slated for ordinary schools.[28]

In addition, the key middle schools visited reported declining enrollments since 1978, when the system was officially restored and the secondary school entrance examinations reintroduced. The cutback in enrollments is said to be necessary to guarantee quality and is part of the transformation back to keypoint status for these schools. Among the sharpest reductions were those reported by the Number Two Middle School affiliated with the East China Teachers' Training University (Shanghai) and the Nanjing Teachers' Training College Affiliated Middle School. In 1978 the former had some thirty-eight classes of students. By the 1980-81 academic year, the number had been cut to twenty-two classes. The size of each class was also in the process of being reduced from about 60 to 40 students each. Similarly, the Nanjing school was cutting back from fifty-six classes to thirty. Nankai Middle School in Tianjin had as many as seventy classes with 4,000 students at one point after classes resumed in the late 1960s, but had by the 1979-80 academic year only forty classes with 1,898 students.

Concentration of Resources. The concentration of resources within the keypoint stream was intensified during the latter half of 1980, with a national movement to make the keypoint system more efficient by reducing in substance the number of such schools at all levels. The greater concentration of resources in an even smaller number of key universities than were initially so designated was mentioned in the Preface. The decision to do the same at the secondary level was a major focus of the National Keypoint Middle Schools Work Conference convened in Ha'erbin in late July 1980. The conference site was appropriate since Heilongjiang province was apparently among the pioneers of this movement almost a year earlier.[29]

As the ministry spokesman had noted in discussing the key universities, the official accounts all claimed that each locality had initially designated too many middle and primary schools as keypoints. Human, material, and financial resources were thus still spread too thinly among them, and the key schools were not really keypoints in substance. Hence the selection of a smaller number of the very best schools wherein the resources of any given locality could be allocated in even more concentrated form.

The city of Tianjin provided the most details. After selecting out twenty-seven key middle schools and forty-five key primaries from among the original group of sixty-six and ninety-one, respectively, Tianjin announced that the following seven measures were being implemented to accomplish the concentration.

(1) Administrative reorganization was the first order of business. Whereas previously some of these schools had been run by the city and some by its districts, all in the smaller group were designated city keypoints. But within this smaller group of seventy-two key schools, six (five secondary and one primary) were brought under the direct administration of the Tianjin Education Bureau. The remaining sixty-six schools were placed under joint city and district leadership.

(2) Starting with the six schools managed by the city alone, the existing contingent of leadership cadres was to be replenished with young and middle-aged personnel who understood both teaching and school administration. Within a few months of this announcement made in mid-1980, it was reported that the administration of all twenty-seven key middle schools had already been augmented by the transfer of forty-four experienced teachers to leadership work. More than 90 percent of the leading cadres in these schools were said to be professional educators.

(3) Within two years, according to the goal set in mid-1980, at least 75 percent of all teachers in the seventy-two schools should be college graduates or the equivalent. In pursuit of this goal, 319 such teachers were transferred into these schools by the autumn semester.

(4) Also within two years, all senior sections of the key middle schools were to complete the change-over from a two-year to a three-year system.

(5) The number of classes in each school was to be limited. Complete key secondary schools could have no more than thirty classes of students, or four classes per year for each of the three junior middle years and six classes per year at the senior level. Those schools that taught only the senior level were limited to a maximum of twenty-four classes of students. Key primary schools could enroll only four classes per grade and were not to run attached junior secondary classes as was commonly done in the 1970s.

(6) Within two years, each key secondary school was to have equipped six to eight biology, physics, and chemistry laboratories, a library, and a classroom with audio-visual teaching aids. Each key primary school was to have outfitted special facilities for library reading, science activities, music, general knowledge, and an audio-visual classroom.

(7) In order to guarantee the quality of the students, the five key middle schools were to enroll the best students from the entire city; the remaining schools would recruit the best from within their own districts only. The forty-five key primary schools were to enroll the best students within the boundaries of their own school districts.[30]

Among the localities to announce similar concentrations of resources and effort within their keypoint school systems at this time were: Beijing, with plans to concentrate on the development of only 32 of the original 117 key primary and secondary schools named in 1978; Guangdong, which reduced the number of its provincial-level key middle schools from 20 to 16; Sichuan, which chose to concentrate on 41 key middle schools and 250 key primaries from among the original group of 300 and 400, respectively; Guizhou province, which singled out 20 key middle schools for special attention from the original group of 131; Shandong, which decided to "improve groups of selected key middle schools in turn," concentrating initially on only 19; and Fujian, which chose to concentrate on 112 of the total 300 key primary schools run by all levels—provincial, city, prefectural, county, and district—but with a much smaller group of only 16 schools chosen to be developed first.[31]

Pass Rates into College. The chief task of the key middle schools, as acknowledged by everyone, is to prepare students for college, and the education they provide has now been reoriented solely toward that aim. University administrators all asserted that a majority of their students are coming from these key middle schools, although no statistics were offered in support of the claim. But the middle schools themselves all referred to their rising pass rates into college as the chief indicator of their renewed excellence by comparison with other schools.

One teacher from an ordinary Shanghai middle school confirmed for another researcher the same process, albeit from the opposite perspective. More than thirty students from this school successfully competed for college enrollment when the first post-Cultural Revolution unified entrance exams were given in 1977. In 1978, after this school had lost some of its best students to the district keypoint schools, its successful college candidates were just over twenty in number. By 1979 the figure was down to around ten.[32]

Among the key schools, however, the figures are all moving upward and, as their administrators pointed out, are well above the national average. In the late 1970s, pass rates *(shengxuelu)* were calculated most commonly as the percentage of those taking the examinations who actually enter college. The national average, when adjusted to include expanded or extra-quota enrollments, rose from 4.87 percent in 1977 to 7.81 percent in 1980, as shown in table 2 (p. 125). Most of the schools visited were still in the process of transition to keypoint status, and their graduating classes of 1979 and 1980 did not all fully reflect the competitive advantage anticipated from the newly restored senior secondary school entrance exams.

Hence Nankai Middle School in Tianjin, which claimed pass rates of 70-80 percent prior to the Cultural Revolution, could boast only 20 percent in 1979. At Lanzhou Middle School Number Twenty-eight that same year, only 160 members of the graduating class took the college entrance exams, of whom 29 (18 percent) were successful. At Chengdu Middle School Number Seven, the pass rate was 11 percent in 1978 and 15 percent in 1979.

The 1980 pass rates for other schools were all substantially higher: 38 percent for the Nanjing Teachers' Training College Affiliated Middle School (where only 225 of the 417 graduating seniors took the exams); 42 percent at Jinan Middle School Number Twenty-two (62 percent including students subsequently enrolled in newly formed, tuition-paying courses for commuter college students); 67 percent at Xiamen Middle School Number Eight; and 99 percent at East China Teachers' Training University's affiliated school (where all but three of the 241 graduating seniors took the college entrance examinations and all but one were successful).

The schools would not reveal their standing in the intraprovincial rank order based on these pass rates, however. This information circulates internally and the leading schools vie with one another for the top spots, while those further down the line use it as a measure against which to judge themselves. This kind of competition was severely criticized during the Cultural Revolution, and reflecting the continuing critique of this practice, administrators refused to reveal the rank order publicly, "since education is supposed to be judged by things more important than pass rates." This homily appeared a bit out of place within the context of the multifaceted selection and preparation process that has been re-created with the single aim of producing successful college candidates. Thus, one school could not resist revealing that it was "among the top three in the province," while another also had only two rivals worth mentioning —with reference, in both instances, to college pass rates.

Secondary School Enrollment. As suggested, perhaps the most important feature of the preparatory process is secondary school recruitment itself. It is designed to differentiate and select students solely on the basis of their performance in examinations, which once again dominate school life. These include daily quizzes in some courses and tests at the end of each lesson, in addition to the formal midterms and finals which all schools are required to give each semester from the primary grades upwards. These culminate in the graduation and entrance examinations which determine exit and entry at each level: from primary to junior middle; from junior to senior middle; and from senior middle to college. Though various kinds of tests and examinations continued to be given during the Cultural Revolution decade, they were allowed to play little or no role in determining the progress of a student's academic career. It is this role which has now been restored to them.

Students are channeled into the hierarchy of secondary schools on the basis of their entrance exam scores, although the process varies slightly from place to place and even between districts within the same city. But the objective everywhere is to concentrate the highest-scoring students in the few best middle schools in each locality. A majority of such students originate in keypoint primary schools or the keypoint classes of ordinary primary schools.

Junior secondary school entrance examinations are usually limited to the two subjects of Chinese language and mathematics. Those students whose teachers and parents anticipate that they are potential high-scorers will be advised to apply for admission to keypoint schools, to which entrance is now strictly governed by a system of fixed quotas similar to that for university enrollment.

Primary school graduation exams sometimes double as entrance exams for admission to junior middle school. Where this is so, such examinations are not written by the primary schools but are unified on an all-district or all-city basis by the local education bureau. Most commonly, however, there are two separate sets of exams: one governing graduation from primary school and a second for entrance to junior middle. Of the cities visited, only Lanzhou allowed the key middle school in each district to write its own junior secondary entrance exam. And only Lanzhou gave a second, separate entrance exam for admission to ordinary schools, which all students, including those who failed to enter the keypoints, were required to pass in order to continue their studies.

The entrance to the senior middle level is similarly controlled and determined. The subjects tested are politics and Chinese language (sometimes combined into a single exam); physics and chemistry (also sometimes combined); mathematics; and sometimes a foreign language. A national secondary school entrance examination was considered briefly, according to one school principal, but the idea was abandoned as impractical.

Of the provinces visited, only Fujian claimed to be giving the same senior secondary school entrance exam throughout the province, although the top key schools enrolled at most on an all-prefectural basis. But only Jiangsu was actually trying to unify enrollment province-wide. Entrance exams there were still unified no higher than the city and prefecture. But in 1980 Jiangsu's four leading middle schools each enrolled one experimental class of fifty students at the senior level drawn from among the highest-scoring candidates in the province as a whole. If the experiment proves successful, province-wide enrollment will be expanded for these four schools. One is the Nanjing Teachers' Training College affiliated school, and the other three are the leading middle schools in each of three cities: Yangzhou, Suzhou, and Changzhou.

Resistance. Interestingly, some individuals and schools are resisting this national development of keypoint schools, much as they resisted the opposite trend during the Cultural Revolution decade. Then, parents and schools devised their own informal strategies for preserving something of the substance of the keypoint system, thereby subverting the egalitarian spirit of that period.[33] Similar "subversive" actions are occurring today among ordinary schools trying to preserve something of their recently acquired gains against the overwhelming pressure to divest them thereof.

One college administrator/parent described the struggle developing with his son's primary school teacher. The boy was in his final year of primary school and was one of its best students, near the top of his keypoint class. The school, however, was an ordinary one which still had a junior middle section attached. This circumstance was in itself an indication of local resistance to the current national trend to eliminate these attached junior middle sections. Because the boy was such a good student, the teacher was trying to keep him for the school. As an inducement, she had promised to oversee his future studies personally. But the parents doubted that she had the qualifications to provide tutoring at the secondary level, since she herself had not studied beyond senior middle school. Apparently not certain that they were not treading on potentially dangerous ground, the parents were "trying to convince" the boy to opt for the safer academic course of applying to a city keypoint middle school with a more assured pass rate into college. The parents in this case were themselves first-generation college graduates, the father having been raised by his widowed poor-peasant mother in an old guerrilla base area during the 1940s.

In this same city, moreover, administrators at one of the best key middle schools complained that the ordinary schools had so strongly opposed the prescribed plan of transferring their best teachers out that it essentially had to be abandoned. The city education bureau decided instead simply to assign the best of the new college graduates as they became available each year to teach in the keypoint middle schools. And it was indicated that this city was also among those refusing to cut back on its junior secondary enrollments. Yet despite such successes, the most that individuals, schools, and cities had been able to do, at least up until late 1981, was to devise these limited strategies for minimizing their losses within the overall reversal of national policy back to the keypoint system.

In late 1981, however, a controversy that had never completely disappeared in Chinese education circles after 1976, having to do with the related practices of streaming and the competitive drive to achieve high pass rates, escalated into open criticism of keypoint schools themselves. The commentary echoed in content, if not intensity, the Cultural Revolution critique of these schools and represents the only time that any such statements concerning them have appeared in the press since 1976.

One writer listed three reasons for recommending the abolition once again of the key schools: (1) they could not contribute to raising the general quality of education because they depressed the enthusiasm for learning of the great majority of teachers and students in ordinary schools, just to benefit the minority in the keypoints; (2) they were not beneficial to the all-around development of the nation's talent because they encouraged the one-sided emphasis on pass rates to the detriment of learning; and (3) they were bad for the general development of education because they wasted financial and material resources.[34]

A writer in Shanghai also blamed the concentration of the best students and teachers in the key schools for the declining morale and quality of ordinary schools. And this the writer in turn attributed to the fact that 70 percent of Shanghai's junior secondary graduates were unable to pass their entrance exams and gain admission to senior middle schools in the autumn of 1981.[35] A third writer declared flatly that the difference between keypoint and non-keypoint schools was essentially the same as that between preparing for college and preparing for a life of labor. Yet another commentator deplored the consequent disintegration of the neighborhood-school system created during the 1966-76 decade.[36]

As of early 1982, the controversy clearly had not been settled. Foreign visitors in Shanghai, Guangzhou, and Beijing during the winter of 1981-82 were told that those three cities had decided to abolish key schools at the primary level.[37] But at the same time, the head of the Beijing Municipal Education Bureau declared in print that despite the controversy, which he acknowledged, running keypoint schools was the correct policy and there should be no vacillation in its implementation. He recommended only that a conscientious effort be made to solve the problems associated with key schools and that similar attention be devoted to the proper administration of ordinary schools as well.[38] Following this statement, the debate ceased to be aired in the press.

The head of the Guangzhou Education Bureau elaborated briefly on the controversy that was nevertheless continuing "in society," during a visit to Hong Kong in March 1982. She told this writer that Guangzhou had decided *not* to follow the Shanghai example. For the time being, Guangzhou was to retain its keypoint schools at all levels—unlike Shanghai which had responded to the widespread criticism of the elitism inherent in these schools by transforming them at the primary level. Thus Shanghai's key primary schools had been transformed into "central" *(zhongxin)* schools, a variant at the primary school level that existed in many places, including Shanghai, before and during the Cultural Revolution. The main difference between the two kinds of schools is that the key school represents a concentration of the best personnel, students, and facilities and has no function other than to maintain its own excellence by comparison with ordinary schools. The central school also concentrates resources but, by contrast, has additional administrative and leadership functions with respect to the ordinary schools in its district. One responsibility, for example, is teacher training; the central school's administrators and teachers must organize and lead the others in the district, and course preparation is done collectively *(jiti beike)*. Another difference is that the key school enrolls only the best students from its district, while the central school is supposed to enroll all students who live in the immediate vicinity of the school regardless of ability.

Guangzhou had decided not to follow the Shanghai example immediately because Guangzhou's key primary schools were themselves not yet sufficiently developed in terms of physical resources and teacher quality to take on the extra responsibilities. The bureau chief acknowledged that the national debate and criticism of keypoint schools was continuing but indicated also that the Shanghai case was more a change of names than of substance.

Given the investment in the construction of new buildings and in material acquisitions as well as the reassignment of the better teachers to the keypoint institutions during the past five years, it remains to be seen just where this controversy will lead in practice. It is possible that the proclaimed abolition of key primary schools is intended as little more than a gesture aimed at quieting the widespread criticism of these schools now circulating "in society." If it is to amount to more than this, then a concerted effort would have to be made to distribute these facilities fairly in working-class as well as white-collar neighborhoods, and in general to prevent the central schools from being monopolized by the children of intellectuals, cadres, and those with connections as is now common practice. It should also be pointed out that the gesture to address the problems of keypoint primary schools has not been duplicated at the secondary level where the criticism has been most intense.

Moreover, the related contradictions inherent in the system that inspired the continuing controversy over streaming, pass rates, and keypoint schools remained unresolved and were actually intensifying in various ways by late 1981, as indicated by: (1) the declining secondary school enrollment figures; and (2) the conversion of ordinary schools for vocational training. These developments have redefined the context of the debate since they have significantly changed the nature of the national student body during the past five years.

Thus in 1981, there were at least 14 million fewer students in secondary school than had been enrolled in 1979. All had been factored out of the school system by their low scores on the secondary school entrance exams. This most drastic version of streaming has reduced the difficulties created by teaching students of widely differing aptitudes, which was officially said to have made conventional streaming necessary in the late 1970s, despite the controversy that has always accompanied this practice. With the "worst" students that the Cultural Revolution's development of mass education brought into the system now removed altogether, the more conventional segregation into fast, average, and slow ability groups introduced in 1977-78 could easily be abandoned. Many localities claim to have done just that, following criticism of the practice made by the Education Minister himself in late 1981.[39] Hence the present system can formally bow to the widespread criticism of streaming and reintegrate classrooms, albeit at the cost of significantly reduced enrollments. In fact, the kinds of students who were in the slow streams in 1977-78 were not in school at all by 1981-82.

Similarly, the conversion of non-key general middle schools into technical and vocational institutions, in combination with the closure of many schools, leaves the keypoint senior secondary school standing alone as the only college preparatory stream. This transformation, if fully implemented, would render the term "keypoint" redundant, at least at the senior secondary level, making it possible to eliminate the elitist connotations inherent in the name without changing the elitist nature of the schools themselves.

In the meantime, whether current efforts to overcome the intense cramming and competition are serious enough to modify these practices as junior middle graduates strive for admission to the college preparatory senior middle stream remains to be seen. To date there are no incentives strong enough to induce educators, students, and parents to modify significantly the newly revived national institution of preparing for the entrance examinations to the next level, be it junior middle, senior middle, or college. This is (1) because preparation—described in the following chapter—has demonstrated ability to push up exam scores; and (2) because the shrinking number of places in secondary schools together with the ever-scarce seats in college continue to be awarded primarily on the basis of these scores. In fact, the emphasis on high scores is actually intensifying with the universities now being permitted greater freedom to select high-scoring students outside the confines of the fixed enrollment quota system.

CHAPTER II

Preparation: Reviewing for the College Entrance Exams

"From the time students enter this school," commented an administrator at one of China's most famous middle schools, "the objective is to help them get into college." In terms of specific preparation for the college entrance examinations *(gaokao fuxi)*, this process begins with the separation of those students who wish to take the liberal arts section of the examinations from the others. In the middle schools visited, only one in ten students at most was choosing this option, typically becoming part of a single small class. This separation was occurring most frequently at the start of the senior year, during which all students study only those subjects tested on the college entrance exams. For the liberal arts candidates, these subjects are: politics, Chinese, math, history, geography and a foreign language. For science and engineering candidates, the subjects now are: politics, Chinese, math, physics, chemistry, biology, and a foreign language. Biology was added to the exams in 1981.

The Education Ministry has stipulated that senior secondary students should be separated into these two liberal arts and science streams, but precisely when and how this division should take place is still the subject of widespread debate, reflecting earlier strictures against this practice. The possibilities experimented with since 1978 are to separate students: (1) from the start of their first year of senior middle school; (2) from the start of the second and final year—the most common option reported at the schools visited in 1980; (3) from the start of the final semester of the senior year; and (4) from the start of actual review work for the examinations sometime during that final semester. The restoration of the third year of senior middle school (just beginning in 1980) offers additional options, as does the possibility of adopting an elective course system for the senior students (which was also being considered as of 1980).

In non-keypoint middle schools, students were also being streamed by ability during the final year, if not before, with the better students being organized into separate keypoint or college preparatory classes. In keypoint schools where the senior students had not been uniformly enrolled by the new secondary school entrance exams, students were also being streamed in this manner. Other schools claimed this step to be unnecessary since their students already represented the best in the city or district as determined by the unified entrance examinations.

For example, in the spring of 1980 the graduating class at the Lanzhou middle school had not been enrolled by the new secondary school entrance exams. The senior students were therefore divided into three kinds of classes: (1) the best science students; (2) the ordinary science students; and (3) the liberal arts students. There was, in addition, a fourth kind of class, the *buxiban*, or "make-up class," with sixty tuition-paying (10 *rmb* per semester) students who were repeating the final year's work in preparation for a second try at the entrance exams. Schools are now officially encouraged to run such make-up classes if local conditions permit.

The Review Process and Materials

Review and preparation work for the examinations follows a more or less set pattern. This preparatory work became the focus first of intense interest in an effort to discover the most effective formulas for success, and then of intense controversy once the consequences of those formulas became apparent.

According to the pattern most frequently reported, the review process usually occupies the three months prior to the examinations, which are held each year in July. In fact, all manner of variations on this pattern are possible: one school reported that its keypoint, or "fast," classes were allowed to devote the whole last semester to reviewing for the examinations. The entire city of Changchun was reported to be doing the same thing, and critical press comments indicate that some schools were actually using most of the senior year for that purpose.[1]

Most schools visited, however, reported that regular course work is completed for the graduating seniors during the first month of their final semester, that is, by the end of March. In one school, there then followed a two-month systematic review of the senior secondary curriculum in preparation for the unified city-wide graduation exams. Students passing these then embarked upon a month-long review session prior to the July examinations.[2]

As noted, the graduation exam is now frequently doubling as the preliminary qualifying examination for college. Even when this is not the case, however, students doing poorly at this stage are being discouraged in one way or another from attempting the July examinations. One of the many burdens falling upon the principal teachers or "class masters" *(banzhuren)* of the graduating classes at this time has been that of "mobilizing" the poorer students to withdraw voluntarily from the competition. But such students apparently cannot be barred on academic grounds from taking the examinations if they insist on doing so. These students may only be prevented from taking the written exams if they fail to achieve the status of senior middle school graduates. This is determined by both the results of the graduation exam and the regular course grades for the senior year.

The Nanjing middle school reported, for instance, that in 1980 its senior class contained 417 students, of whom 20 were not permitted to graduate. These latter were simply sent away at the end of the year with a school-leaving instead of a graduation certificate. Yet only 225 of the graduating seniors actually took the college entrance exams that year.

Former teachers interviewed in Hong Kong spoke of efforts to dissuade the poorer students from attempting the college entrance exams so as to prevent them from adversely affecting the school's pass rate. They also spoke of internal revisions in the manner of calculating the pass rates in order to discourage such pressuring. The proposed method would have calculated each school's pass rate as a percentage of the entire graduating class rather than only of those taking the exam. But the proposal appears to have fallen by the wayside. This particular problem is now being approached from a different direction, however, with the systematic effort to reduce the number of candidates. The preliminary qualifying exams thus serve to disqualify the low-scoring students automatically, as does the increasingly effective preselection of high-scoring students by channeling them via the system of unified examination and enrollment into the hierarchy of keypoint secondary schools.

Another variation of the review process is to administer the graduation exams early, as was being done in Fujian province. An entire three months was thereby made available for preparatory work, which included at least one quality assessment *(zhiliang jiancha)*. This is in effect a mock examination, unified on an all-city or prefectural basis, which is used to rank the schools and graduating classes in various ways. The purpose is to demonstrate their strengths and weaknesses on the examination subjects in order to assist them in their preparatory work.

The famous Middle School Number Eight in Xiamen described its preparatory work as a sort of hand-crafted process, wherein each graduating senior's abilities in the various exam subjects are carefully monitored. This is done by the school's best teachers and coordinated by the class master of each graduating class. Virtually all those assigned to this work are older teachers with experience dating back to the pre-1966 years, or younger teachers trained by their older colleagues. Some, it was noted, have grown so skilled over the years that they are able to predict with remarkable accuracy—independent of any insiders' tips—the questions and essay topics which appear on the college entrance exams each year.

In 1980 the four graduating classes at this middle school contained only 179 students, all of whom took the July examinations. These students had not been formally streamed into ability groups, since the 1980 seniors were already supposed to represent the best students in the Xiamen urban and suburban area. Only 120 passed the exams, however. For all of the students, their graduation exams in March had been followed by the quality assessment.

Review work then began on 10 April and continued until the national examinations, given that year from 7 to 9 July. The first six weeks of this period were devoted to a review of basic knowledge that covered all of the prescribed examination subjects in accordance with the general review outline published by the Education Ministry. Then followed two weeks of summing up, answering practice questions, and writing sample essays, this last in preparation for the important composition section which accounts for 40 percent of the grade on the Chinese language exam. During the remaining weeks, the candidates studied on their own.

Throughout the period, the teachers were continuously evaluating the students' capabilities in relation to the review outlines and sample questions so as to fill in any gaps and strengthen weak areas. Administrators at this school would not admit to segregating the very brightest seniors into a special group or class, called *jianziban* (literally, "sharpies' class"), as some schools do. Teachers instead followed the practice of *yincai shijiao*, or teaching according to the aptitude of each individual student. Those able to move at a faster pace than their peers were encouraged to do so with extra and more difficult review assignments. Here, too, the most experienced teachers assigned to this guidance work are said to have near perfect records in identifying the students most likely to succeed.

The review materials are another item of keen interest. The first of these was the *Review Outline for the National College Entrance Examinations*, a pamphlet published annually by the Ministry of Education. This small booklet of no more than forty pages outlined in some detail the scope of each subject exam and served as the basis for the plethora of supplementary review materials prepared by provinces, cities, and individual schools. The Ministry stopped issuing this outline after 1980, since it was regarded as only a transitional necessity given the widely varying standards obtaining in the immediate wake of the Cultural Revolution.[3] Review materials are now based on the national unified secondary school curriculum, textbooks, and teaching materials, which also serve as the sole basis for the college entrance exam questions. The reunification of the secondary school curriculum and teaching materials following the decentralization of the Cultural Revolution decade was completed by the 1980-81 academic year.

The locally published review materials include elaborations and explanations of the review outline for each subject; questions drawn from past exams, together with the answers and the weight or number of points given to each question; and individual books summarizing the essential information for each examination subject. In addition, provinces with low performance ratings will reprint materials prepared in the high-scoring provinces. Those prepared by Fujian, for example, are reputed to be among the best and are in great demand —reflecting that province's outstanding performance on the examinations over the years. A popular edition such as this may sell out quickly and then be reproduced in various ways by individuals who sell the material privately or as a cooperative venture—often at prices much higher than the original. Indeed, so keen is the competition and so serious the process of preparation that each candidate typically collects "many tens" of such books and pamphlets. Published "letters to the editor" and the authorities themselves have warned about the dangers of relying on some of these unauthorized editions which include not only reprints but locally compiled materials complete with inflated claims and prices to match. But no concerted effort has yet been made to curtail their publication.[4]

Middle schools also have compiled their own materials and sample questions over the years. Such materials are supposed to be kept "secret" and circulate only among the school's own students. But there is naturally much demand for the review materials compiled by schools with a history of high pass rates.

Learning from Fujian

Fujian's review procedures and materials have come under close national scrutiny due to that province's otherwise inexplicable performance on the college entrance examinations. And herein lies a morality tale of no little complexity. It illustrates the issues both that inspired one of the Cultural Revolution's main critiques of education and that continue to create controversy in Chinese education today. Thus no sooner had Fujian's high scores been acclaimed and analyzed than it became necessary to suppress public discussion of the findings. To the embarrassment of the present leadership, they verified the Cultural Revolution critique which, stripped of its political rhetoric, has wide appeal among progressive educators everywhere. This suppression of the causes and consequences of Fujian's achievement made it necessary to piece the story together from administrators around the country since those at Fujian's leading university "could not" discuss it.

Fujian's reputation as a national examinations standard-bearer did not begin until the late 1950s. But from that time until the Cultural Revolution, Fujian's provincial pass rate was always among the top eight in the country. This performance revived immediately in the post-Cultural Revolution era, with Fujian achieving the highest minimum passing score in 1978 and 1979 on the first two nationally unified entrance examinations (those given in 1977 were unified only at the provincial level).

It should be noted that the provincial minimum passing score (hereafter, mps) is not an average score but rather a statement of the relationship between the provincial quota of college freshmen and the top scores achieved. Thus, if a province's quota is 10,000, the top-scoring 10,000 candidates in the province will be allowed to pass regardless of their absolute scores, plus a certain margin added for administrative purposes. The margin is the subject of another controversy described below. In effect, then, the mps is derived from the lowest score achieved by the top 10,000 candidates in the province.

In 1978, Fujian had an mps of 365 points in science and 340 points in liberal arts, out of a maximum 500 points possible.[5] By contrast, Fujian's neighbors, Jiangxi and Guangdong, scored much lower. Jiangxi had an mps of 320 points for liberal arts and 300 points for the sciences, while Guangdong's mps hovered around 300 points as well.[6] Fujian's achievement was all the more impressive since the 1966-76 decade was reputed to have been particularly disruptive there, and also because this generally backward province had so clearly upstaged the intellectual and cosmopolitan centers of the country, namely, Shanghai, Beijing, Zhejiang, and Jiangsu.

A recheck of the 1978 scores was conducted, and after the 1979 results were in, the Education Ministry instructed universities that enrolled high-scoring Fujian students to monitor their grades in regular course work by comparison with their peers. The findings, as reported by several of these universities, were that the outstanding scores achieved by Fujian candidates on the college entrance examinations were not matched by similarly outstanding grades on their subsequent college course work.

At Nankai University, for example, the Fujian students were found to be "just a little above average" but not markedly so. As a group, they were not among the university's best students. Fudan University reported that although Fujian students as a whole had scored higher than the Shanghai students on the entrance examinations, the latter generally achieved higher grades in college courses thereafter. Similar findings were reported at Shandong and Nanjing Universities and by the Education Ministry spokesman as well.

According to all these administrators, the conclusion that has been drawn from these findings is that Fujian's high scores must be related to the intensive and systematic nature of the preparatory work done in that province. Of particular importance is thought to be the use of most of the final semester for review and the experienced teachers assigned to guide the work. A lengthy analysis published in *Guangming ribao* following the 1978 exams also traced Fujian's success to its preparatory work. This analysis focused—with approval—on the use of the "keypoint" concept in the province's secondary schools. The concept was being applied not only to individual schools, but to individual classes within schools, and ultimately to the brightest students *(jianzi xuesheng)* within classes, who were given special tutoring to enable them "to achieve the level of their capabilities."[7]

In Fujian itself, the systematic nature of the preparation process for the examinations is associated with the tenure of Wang Yugeng as head of the provincial bureau of education from 1954 to 1966.[8] She is famous in Fujian education circles as the chain-smoking, no-nonsense wife of the then provincial First Party Secretary, Ye Fei. She took upon herself the task of improving Fujian's performance record. This she did according to the methods and standards of the time, by emphasizing the keypoints of educational development in the main coastal towns—notably, Fuzhou, Putian, Chuanzhou, Jimei, and Xiamen—where a number of well-known schools had been established and financed by Overseas Chinese. She personally visited these schools to encourage the "red flag" competitions between classes within schools and between schools in a variety of unified tests and assessments. The competitions were based on examination pass rates and culminated each year in the national college entrance examinations.

Such methods, of course, constituted one of the main inspirations for the Cultural Revolution critique of Chinese education, and Wang Yugeng was duly criticized for her efforts at mass Red Guard rallies. By 1980, she had reportedly given up smoking and was a deputy Party secretary at the Beijing Teachers' Training University. But in Fujian, people were "still thinking about her methods," as were educators throughout the country. Several acknowledged that "everyone is now learning from Fujian."

Even Shanghai, rarely made to feel insecure in its assumptions of intellectual superiority, sent a group to the province to investigate the methods used there to prepare candidates for the college entrance exams. And the Education Ministry spokesman, recalling the Cultural Revolution critique of such competition, cramming, and ranking, laughed at the irony that everyone was now trying to emulate Fujian's methods for "stuffing ducks." They continued to do so in both Shanghai and Beijing even after the university investigations had shown that students from those two cities did better in regular course work than those from Fujian, despite the higher scores the latter were able to achieve on the entrance examinations. Meanwhile, Fujian educators are amused by the national scramble to learn the secrets of their success. Fujian's high-scoring keypoint middle schools refuse to reveal the details of their review methods even to their own "fraternal" *(xiongdi)* schools within the home province, much less to outsiders from Shanghai.

The universities claim to disapprove of the great emphasis on exam preparation. But one Zhongshan University administrator highlighted the contradiction inherent in his disapproval by saying, almost in the same breath, that "Guangdong is willing to take more Fujian students because they earn such high marks on the college entrance exams."

In 1980, however, Fujian's ranking slipped from first to seventh place. Since the practice is now officially discouraged, the rank order could not be publicized, although it was informally revealed that Zhejiang, Jiangsu, and Jiangxi came in first, second, and third, respectively, in terms of provincial mps. School administrators in Fujian indicated that the sudden decline was then under investigation. They suggested that with the new more difficult curriculum, Fujian's four-year secondary school system was finding it increasingly difficult to compete with provinces that had a five-year system. But educators elsewhere suggested that, since everyone else was adopting Fujian's preparation methods, the province would simply have to try that much harder in the future to maintain its high rating.

Confronting the Contradictions

The contradictions inherent in the story recounted above deserve elaboration. Educators disapprove of excessive emphasis on exam preparation, yet they actively seek to enroll the students with the highest exam scores. Provinces vie with each other to push up their minimum passing scores, but the public announcement of the provincial rank order is forbidden. The entire country rushed to learn the secrets of Fujian's success, but educators in Fujian could not discuss it. These contradictions indicate the controversies that have continued within Chinese education circles since the entrance exams were restored. The initial "leftist" outburst against the exams, which was expressed in clearly political terms, was quickly subdued.[9] Thereafter, criticism focused on the permissible areas of the physical and psychological strains created by the examinations. The 1978 press accounts were full of eager youths encouraged by conscientious teachers. The heroes that year were people like the middle school physics teacher in Fujian. Suffering from a recurrence of tuberculosis, he had to be ordered into a hospital bed, from which he doggedly continued to work on lecture notes and preparatory materials.[10]

A distinct change appeared in 1979, however, when the public focus shifted to the tensions the examinations were generating: schools devoting the entire senior year to exam preparation; students themselves drawing up daily cram schedules that went nonstop from 6:00 a.m. to 10:30 p.m.; and parents telling their children not to return home if they failed to gain admission to college. As luck would have it, while reporters were collecting material for such a story at one middle school, a physics teacher there collapsed and died. The cause, it was said, was overwork. Also criticized as disruptive of the learning process when used to excess were the various unified city and district quality assessments used for ranking purposes in preparation for the college entrance examinations, as described above.[11]

It was generally acknowledged that the cause of all these problems and more was the single-minded pursuit, not of learning, but of a school's pass rate into college.[12] The critique reached a crescendo of sorts in 1980, when it was officially sanctioned in a five-point recommendation made by Vice-Minister of Education Zhang Chengxian at a National Work Conference on Keypoint Middle Schools. The five specific points were:

(1) Nationally, stop ranking the provinces according to their scores on the college entrance exams; similarly, within provinces, cities, and counties, stop ranking middle schools on the basis of their scores; do not use the pass rate into college as the sole criterion for judging whether or not a school is doing its work well; and stop giving out rewards and penalties to schools and teachers based on the numbers of their students admitted to college—a widely reported practice in the late 1970s following the new emphasis on individual material incentives in other sectors.

(2) Liberate the schools and students from excessive examinations; schools should give only midterms and finals, while the provinces, prefectures, cities, counties, and districts should not give unified quality assessments and other tests for ranking purposes.

(3) Adhere strictly to the teaching plan and syllabus, and do not try to finish early by crash-course methods in order to leave more cramming time for the college entrance exams.

(4) Do not ignore the majority of the students in order to concentrate efforts only on the graduating classes and the especially bright *(jianzi)* students within them.

(5) Guarantee that students preparing for the college entrance exams have nine hours of sleep each night.[13]

Just what level of rigor is to be applied in the implementation of these measures *(cuoshi)* is not yet clear. As with so many other regulations in education, these appear to be in the nature of general guidelines which allow substantial leeway for local interpretation. Even if only superficially implemented, the measures would at least serve to soften the appearance of cramming and competition gone to excess; but whether the reality will be appreciably modified remains to be seen. Some educators indicated that a similar situation existed in the mid-1960s, when official strictures also existed against cramming, excessive competition, and rank ordering on the basis of pass rates. Yet all of these practices continued "internally" behind the façade of progressive official regulations.

The information available to date points to a similar fate for the 1980 measures. Thus, the administrators interviewed all demurred in one way or another on the topic of the provincial mps rank order. Yet everyone knew which provinces were in first, second, and third place, and that Fujian had come in seventh. The five measures outlined above were announced on 4 August, at approximately the same time that the mps were being calculated. But the strictures against provincial rank ordering were clearly not enforced, except for the prohibition placed on public proclamation of it. As for additional national regulations aimed at enforcing the new measures, the only one so far identifiable was a ruling that the 1981 exam include some questions based on the final semester's teaching plan. This was intended to discourage teachers from cutting the school year short to allow more time for cramming.[14]

Locally, the city of Shanghai officially limited the period of preparation to the final six weeks before the exams.[15] And other localities were said to have adopted similar kinds of limitations. But no middle schools visited in 1980 either before or after the new measures were announced acknowledged any concrete practices or confided any plans to alter the basic preparatory process described above. Follow-up press commentaries in 1981 indicated, moreover, that schools and education bureaus around the country were not yet under any great pressure on this account. One report from Shandong described how the practices in question were continuing unabated there. Rural schools were pushing their graduating seniors especially hard, the study day for some of these potential candidates lasting from 4:30 a.m. to 10:00 p.m., Sundays and holidays included.[16]

An account from Shanghai told of continuing pressure from the district education bureaus on the key schools to guarantee 100 percent pass rates; of districts and counties still computing their rank orders; and of penalties and rewards meted out on the basis of the pass rates into college. A certain county middle school was even said to be awaiting the results of the 1982 college entrance examinations before allocating newly constructed staff housing to classroom teachers.[17]

Despite the broadcast announcement of an Education Ministry directive forbidding the use of the 1981 Spring Festival holiday for college entrance exam preparation, education authorities in the city of Dalian decided to ignore the order. The senior secondary graduating classes all worked throughout the holiday as planned. Moreover, the emphasis on the pass rate into college was said to be continuing there as the sole means used by "society," parents, and school leaders to judge the quality of a school's teachers and, specifically, the ability of the individual instructors assigned to the graduating classes.[18]

Yet another report claimed that crash-course methods of preparation were continuing generally. In addition, primary and junior middle schools were engaged in the same exercise, trying to push up the pass rates of their students into junior and senior middle school and especially into key schools at those levels.[19] And two secondary school teachers from Fujian, interviewed in Hong Kong during the summer of 1982 shortly after their arrival there, said that the intensive preparatory process had remained unchanged in their respective counties in 1981.

Unfortunately, it is still not possible to divest this story of the controversy that surrounds it in China and release the results of the pertinent investigations that have been carried out there. These investigations would at the very least illustrate the parallels between the Chinese debate and a similar kind of controversy that has grown up in the United States over the role of preparation in enhancing scores on the widely used examinations provided by the National Testing Service. But given the importance of the college entrance examinations in the "struggle between the two lines" in education, the present Chinese leadership would find it at least embarrassing, and probably politically hazardous as well, to publicize what the Fujian case and the national experience as a whole suggest, namely, that (1) students can be primed to excell in these examinations, and (2) the process can be refined and elevated into a national art; but (3) the process will not necessarily identify the best and brightest talent for college.

That educators in China are fully aware of these points has been demonstrated by their findings on the post-enrollment performance of the high-scoring Fujian students. Everyone is also aware of the harmful effects of the cramming and competition. In 1981, intensifying press criticisms—of the single-minded pursuit of pass rates, of the channeling of primary and middle school students into fast and slow streams primarily for that purpose, and of the keypoint school system itself—all testify to the now official admission of these negative features inherent in the present education system.

Perhaps because it is now politically more secure, the current leadership is willing to acknowledge as it would not in 1977 and 1978 some of the consequences of restoring the pre-1976 education system. Whether this system's harshest effects can be effectively modified by the present piecemeal approach remains to be seen, however, since policy-makers still appear unwilling to admit where the root cause of the problem lies. Hence they continue to push the system in a general direction which, in many respects, is actually intensifying the conditions they now officially claim to want to ameliorate.

For example, the value of a college education has been significantly enhanced since 1976. It has become one of the few secure routes to a well-paying job and a highly respected—some even say glorious—place in Chinese society. The political disadvantages associated with being a college graduate and an intellectual have now been cast aside. No longer tainted as associate members of the bourgeoisie, intellectuals have officially joined the ranks of the laboring people. But unlike many other groups thereof, the iron rice bowl of the college graduate remains unchallenged. Junior secondary school-leavers, and even senior secondary graduates, count themselves fortunate today to be placed in a state-run enterprise or organization with the guaranteed employment, wages, and benefits such a job assignment entails. Even so, their starting salaries will only be in the range of 30-40 *rmb* per month. The college graduate, by contrast, is guaranteed attractive employment conditions, plus all of the guarantees and benefits of a state job, and a starting salary of approximately 50 *rmb* per month, although the new worker bonus systems may now narrow the wage differential fairly quickly for some trades and enterprises.

The value of a college education has also been enhanced by changing political fashions. As will be shown below, "studying well for the four modernizations" has become the key criterion for admission to the Communist Youth League. Although the great majority of college freshmen are CYL members, such membership is not officially a prerequisite for admission. Rather, admission to both college and the CYL are determined primarily by the same criterion: academic excellence. Hence, personal, political, and national self-interest have all been realigned and can now be served by the same end, namely, admission to college.

Meanwhile, college seats continue to be awarded primarily on the basis of entrance exam scores, while the highest-scoring candidates continue to be rewarded with places in the most prestigious key schools. Moreover, the emphasis on high scores is actually increasing, as will also be illustrated in subsequent chapters, with the key universities now enjoying greater freedom to select high-scoring students outside the confines of their fixed enrollment quotas.

Under these circumstances, the current efforts to tone down the most glaring effects of cramming and competition do not appear to offer sufficiently strong incentives to achieve the declared aim. The basic structure of the system remains unchanged and it is designed to reward high pass rates. As if to underscore this fact, a major argument for integrated classrooms in several middle schools where streaming had been dropped was that they were actually found to push up pass rates![20] Nothing must interfere with the aim of promoting them, not even a reform ostensibly designed to discourage the single-minded pursuit of high scores at the expense of learning such as streaming represented within the school system.

Finally, the then Education Minister Jiang Nanxiang himself offered an analysis of the underlying "objective reason" for all of these problems, which appeared only to highlight the growing contradictions within the education system over which he presided. Responding to points of criticism raised by deputies at the National People's Congress meeting in December 1981, the Education Minister agreed—as do educators at all levels throughout the country—that the competition for admission to college was more intense than at any time before the Cultural Revolution. But he explained that the underlying reason for the excessive emphasis on college exam pass rates at the middle school level was the disproportionate development of secondary and tertiary education. He recalled that when the unified college entrance examinations were first introduced in the early 1950s, they did not result in a preoccupation with pass rates since there were not even enough middle school graduates in those early years to meet the demand for college students. It was not until the 1960s, after senior secondary schooling had been significantly expanded, that the various manifestations of the competitive drive for admission to college developed. But even then, he maintained, the annual proportion of senior middle graduates going on to college varied between 30 and 40 percent.

What had changed all this was the rash popularization of senior secondary schooling during the 1966-76 decade. As a result, at present only the top 4-5 percent of each year's senior secondary graduates could gain admission to college. The Minister concluded, not that the "extremely fierce competition" was the consequence of the restored entrance examinations, but that the competition was due to the "unprecedentedly sharp contradiction between the vast numbers of senior middle school graduates and the low university enrollment quotas." And, added Jiang, "the pressure created by the pursuit of a higher percentage of students going on to higher education is the main reason for the excessive burden of work that middle school students must shoulder."[21]

The ratios of college freshmen to which the Education Minister made reference are shown in table 4 (p. 127). If the main purpose is seen as being one of too many candidates chasing too few places in college, then the answer is clearly to reduce the one or increase the other. In this case, the nature of the problem depends on how it is interpreted. Since the latter is limited by economic and physical constraints, the only answer is to reduce the number of potential candidates.

The present Administration appears to have been caught unprepared for the consequences of attempting to superimpose the tracks, streams, and enrollment criteria of the 1950s and 1960s upon the system of mass secondary education inherited from the Cultural Revolution decade. To date, policy-makers have devised a two-pronged solution for the ensuing "contradictions." On the one hand, they have responded in a piecemeal, crisis-management fashion to the widespread criticism of cramming, competition, and streaming. The result has been a series of *ad hoc* measures and exhortations intended to minimize the most glaring effects of these practices. But the extent to which such efforts can succeed remains uncertain, given: the value placed on a college education in Chinese society today; the continuing use of the college entrance examination scores as the chief criterion for admission; and the demonstrated ability of the much-debated preparatory methods to push up those scores.

The second prong of the solution comprises the more substantive measures currently being implemented, that is: (1) the sharp reduction of senior secondary enrollments; (2) the reduction in the number of students admitted to the keypoint middle schools; and (3) the plan to convert the remaining ordinary middle schools into institutions for vocational learning. These measures should indeed go a long way toward solving the basic problem, identified by the Education Minister as too many college candidates. The uncertainty here is a political one, namely, whether he and his successors will be able to convince parents, educators, and the opposition that his analysis of the problem is the correct one, or that the declared ends justify the present means.

CHAPTER III

Eligibility Refinements: Application, Political Assessment, Physical Examination, and Individual Preference

The preparatory paces through which graduating secondary school seniors are put represent an attempt to minimize the uncertainties that the written examinations hold for each candidate. The candidate has even less control over several other elements of the preenrollment process. That process itself has been basically, although not yet entirely, standardized throughout the country. It therefore unfolds in a somewhat different order from one province to another, which in itself means certain arbitrary differential advantages for some students over others.

The process entails four steps: the formal application *(baoming gaokao)*, the political assessment *(zhengzhi shencha)*, the health examination *(shenti jiancha)*, and the completion of the preference form *(zhiyuanbiao)* listing, in order of preference, the schools and majors to which the individual candidate wishes to apply. Before the Cultural Revolution, these four steps were all completed prior to the written examinations. In 1977 and 1978, when several million students took the examinations, the latter three steps in the application process were usually required only of those candidates who actually "passed," that is, achieved the minimum passing score (mps).

With the more recent decline in the number of students taking the entrance examinations, the provinces are gradually reverting to the pre-1966 sequence for reasons of convenience. University administrators anticipate that the old procedure will eventually be uniformly restored since it reduces the pressures of enrollment work. In recent years, virtually all of this has had to be completed during the single month of August following the grading of the examinations, which takes most of July to complete. In the late 1970s, the key universities were required to begin the autumn semester on 1 September; the new date is 10 September. Hence the system is currently in a state of transition and a variety of procedures are being followed throughout the country.

For example, the autonomous cities of Shanghai and Beijing, with fewer absolute numbers of students sitting for the examinations, were among the first to revert to the pre-1966 sequence. Both had completed the transition by 1980. At the same time, some provinces, such as Guangdong, Fujian, and

Zhejiang, were still waiting until after the written examinations to complete the final three steps, and still others were already in the process of transition. Jilin province was requiring candidates to write their individual preference forms prior to the examinations.[1] Jiangsu began in 1980 to conduct the political assessment prior to the written examinations and introduced a preliminary health check for middle school seniors so as to discover at the outset those with major health problems which would automatically disqualify them. The writing of the preference form in Jiangsu remained unchanged in 1980, but it was partially revised the following year.[2]

Shandong had both preliminary health and political checks by 1980. These were conducted by middle schools as a basis for permitting their seniors to take the written examinations, although the formal physical and political assessments were still conducted afterward.[3] In 1981, Guangdong began conducting the political assessments of all graduating middle school seniors and those attending the middle school make-up or prep courses prior to the written examinations; other candidates were assessed afterward.[4]

The significance of the sequence is that in the pre-1966 pattern, some candidates are disqualified for health or political reasons before even attempting the written examinations. In addition, all those taking the exams must write their school preferences based solely on their *anticipated* performance. The immediate post-Cultural Revolution sequence, on the other hand, placed maximum pressure on the administrators responsible for completing all enrollment work within only a few weeks but was fairer to the applicants. This is especially true with respect to the preference form, since knowing how well one has done on the written exams, particularly in relation to everyone else, can be of some benefit to the candidate, as will be explained below.

Administrators also pointed to a few exceptions made with respect to the physical exam in 1977, when many of the rules and regulations were apparently not yet fully operational. Thus, after seeing their outstanding examination scores, some universities admitted people who should, under normal circumstances, have been disqualified from the competition because of physical disabilities.

In summary, the prerequisites for taking the written entrance examinations are now in the process of being refined to include, in addition to the general eligibility requirements mentioned above concerning age, cultural level, marital status, and work unit approval: (1) satisfactory performance on preliminary qualifying examinations and assessments; (2) the absence of serious physical disabilities; and (3) the absence of serious political liabilities.

It is the responsibility either of the middle school (for graduating seniors), the work unit (for those already employed), or the neighborhood street committee (for those in neither category) to ensure that the prerequisites, however locally defined, have been met for each candidate. The various procedures for ascertaining the necessary facts are determined by the provincial education authorities in accordance with the general and internal regulations issued by the Education Ministry.

The public bodies officially charged with interpreting these regulations and adapting them to local conditions are the provincial enrollment committees *(sheng gaoxiao zhaosheng weiyuanhui).* These are formed anew each year and are composed of about twenty persons, mainly provincial-level cadres responsible for culture and education including presidents of universities in the province and the head of the provincial education bureau (or higher education bureau in some provinces). The provincial enrollment committee has decision-making powers with respect to the local implementation of the national regulations, while the actual administrative work is performed by the office *(bangongshi)* of the committee. Both the enrollment committees and their offices are formed by the provincial bureaus of education and are, in effect, a part of those bureaus in a physical as well as a functional sense, since they are typically housed in the same building.

Actually implementing the regulations at the basic level, along with the candidates' sponsoring units, are the county, city, and city-district enrollment offices. These offices are set up each year by the county and city education bureaus, and if sufficient cadres from those bureaus are not available, middle school teachers are seconded for the task. Office staff members return to their own bureaus and schools once enrollment work has been completed each year.

The following discussion of the four main steps of the application process proceeds according to the official post-Cultural Revolution sequence, which was still the most commonly encountered as of 1980. When all of the steps are completed prior to the written exams, as is the case in Shanghai and Beijing, the political and health examinations are conducted first. Those not eliminated by either of these two steps then fill out a preference form together with the formal application. For the sake of coherence, the four main steps of the application process are presented here consecutively, while the examinations themselves have been given separate treatment in the following chapter.

The Formal Application (baoming gaokao)

After all of the preliminaries have been completed, the formal process of applying to sit for the written examinations commences. Once the number of individuals eligible to take the examinations in any given school, work unit, or neighborhood has been ascertained, this information is passed on to the local enrollment office, which provides the appropriate number of application forms. Upon completion, the forms are returned to the office, with the stipulated number of photographs and the fifty-cent (recently raised to 1 *rmb)* application fee which must accompany each application. This procedure is undertaken approximately one month prior to the written examinations. The local enrollment office then issues the necessary examination permit *(zhunkaozheng)* to each candidate, without which he/she may not enter the examination hall.

In addition to such basic information as name, age, sex, and address, students must indicate both their foreign-language choice and their preference regarding either the science or liberal arts exams. Additional details solicited include:

(1) Place of family origin.

(2) Nationality, e.g., Han Chinese, Mongolian, Tibetan, etc.

(3) Status of the applicant *(benren chengfen)*. This refers essentially to the present occupational status of the applicant. Those still in school or who have recently graduated write "student" as their status. This "student" status does not change until after the individual has been permanently established in another occupation and working at it for several years.

(4) Family origin *(jiating chushen)*. This is now interpreted to mean *only* the *present occupation* of the father, a significant change described in detail below.

(5) Whether the applicant is a member of the Communist Party or Youth League.

(6) A short history *(jianli)* of the applicant listing previous schools attended, any work experience, etc.

(7) Whether the candidate has ever received any awards or punishments.

(8) A list of major family members *(jiating zhuyao chengyuan)*, which means primarily parents but includes also elder brothers and sisters and grandparents, particularly if all live together in the same household with the applicant. For each person so listed, the applicant is required to provide the following data: name, relationship, age, work unit, occupation, and political status *(zhengzhi mianmu)*. This last item refers to both the positive and negative factors that comprise "political status," such as whether these persons are now or have ever been members of the Communist Party, the CYL, or any of the minor democratic parties; whether they have committed counterrevolutionary or other crimes, been sentenced to labor reform, etc.; and whether they have any "serious political problems."

(9) Major social relationships *(zhuyao shehui guanxi)*. This requires the same sort of information as is requested for the preceding item but with respect to more distant relatives and other persons with whom the applicant may have had a "direct political or economic relationship."

The candidates themselves must supply all of this information even though it is readily obtainable from middle school records and the registration forms required of graduating seniors *(biyesheng dengjibiao)*. These details constitute the basis of the data used by the candidate's middle school in preparing the political assessment, as will be seen below. The present application form solicits essentially the same information that was required of college applicants both prior to and during the Cultural Revolution decade. The main difference now lies in the changing definition of family origin or class background *(jiating chushen)* and in the differing standards used for evaluating the political/social information provided.

Previously, the term "family origin" referred to the status of the family as determined by the family's *main source of income*. This was in turn determined primarily by the occupation of the principal male member three years prior to liberation (1949) in the cities, or three years prior to land reform whenever that had been carried out in the rural area in question. Throughout most of the Chinese mainland, land reform was carried out sometime between 1947 and 1952. If a family had been designated capitalist at that time, then prior to 1 July 1979, its young members would still have had to declare their family origin to be "capitalist" regardless of the family's present economic circumstances or the occupations of its principal income-earners.

Since 1 July 1979, however, young people are required to indicate only the *occupation (zhiye*, or *chengfen)* of their *fathers* (or the principal income-earner of their immediate family) when asked to declare their family origin *(jiating chushen)*. For the father, however, the old sense of "family origin" has not changed; he must still declare the family's pre-liberation status when asked about his family origin.

Finally, the occupations of members of the capitalist class were previously designated simply as *gongshangye*, or "business and industry." Small-scale operations, also once lumped into this one broad category, are now being differentiated in recognition of their new legitimacy. Thus individuals engaged in a variety of self-employed and family-run enterprises are currently being redesignated as "independent laborers."

The main urban occupations that young people living in cities today are most likely to declare when asked to identify their family origins *(jiating chushen)* are:

(1) Cadre *(ganbu)*, indicating those in positions of administrative and political leadership, including former capitalists now holding such positions. *Geming ganbu*, or "revolutionary cadre," is used to denote those who joined the revolution and the CCP prior to 1949.

(2) White collar *(zhiyuan)*, a comprehensive term indicating all professional people not in leadership positions, for example, schoolteachers, college professors, librarians, research personnel, accountants, interpreters, secretaries *(mishu)*, etc.

(3) Worker *(gongren)*, indicating those engaged in manual labor, including former capitalists if they are now working in this capacity.

(4) Small trader *(xiaoshang)*, which covers self-employed street vendors, food stall operators, repairmen, service workers, etc.; also referred to as "independent laborers."

(5) Handicraft worker *(xiaoshougongyezhe)*, indicating small-scale producers; also referred to as "independent laborers."

In the countryside, young people need no longer identify themselves as belonging to landlord or rich-peasant classes but can declare their family origin to be simply "commune member." The catch here, it might be added, is that *only* people who were formerly in those two categories write "commune member" *(sheyuan)*. Everyone else still writes their "good" old class designations. There is no directive requiring everyone to call themselves commune members in this context.[5]

The Political Assessment (zhengzhi shencha)

This step is the responsibility of the Communist Party organization within the candidate's middle school or work unit. Different localities appear to prepare in marginally different ways the political assessment of "social youth," that is, those neither in school nor employed. Assessments of these candidates will usually be supplied by their parents' work units or their residential neighborhood committees. The political assessment is based on uniform standards whether it is conducted before the written examinations or afterward.

As noted above, the family political and social history included on the college application and secondary school graduation forms constitutes the basis of the information assessed. The graduation registration form also contains, in addition to a grade for each academic subject studied during the senior year, a assessment of the student's own political/deportment record *(biye jianding)*. The latter is a profile or sketch of the individual student—without reference to family background—that is written by the student's main classroom teacher *(banzhuren)*, ideally in consultation with the head of the small group of which each student is a member. Every class, or *ban*, of students is subdivided into a number of small groups, each with an elected leader. The evaluation of its members is supposed to be a consensual decision reached by the small peer group as a whole, which the teacher then officially enters on the student's records. Since the students, as a rule, do not like to speak critically of one another, this assessment is sometimes written by the *banzhuren* alone.

The evaluation covers "political attitude, political consciousness, and moral character" as demonstrated in attitudes toward the Party, social and political matters, labor, study, classmates, and teachers. The evaluation also covers matters of personal conduct, discipline, ability to cooperate, and personal traits which affect interaction with others. Separate columns are reserved for the school authorities' own entries corroborating or elaborating upon this personal classroom record.

These two categories of data—the candidate's personal record and the political, social, and criminal history of the candidate's immediate family, relatives, and close associates—comprise the sum total of the information assessed during the political evaluation for admission to college. It is the responsibility of the Party organization within the candidate's school to ascertain whether the information entered on the graduation and college application forms is accurate, both with respect to the individual and to his/her family and social relations. Work units prepare similar materials on their employees. Personnel from the candidate's school or work unit must go to the parents' place of work or anywhere else necessary to verify the information and thus complete the investigation. In particular, the "serious problems" of a candidate's relatives and associates must be investigated and any necessary supporting materials supplied.[6]

In discussing how this information is used, administrators revealed that there are two main political reasons for disqualifying candidates for admission to college. They are: (1) that the individual candidate had been a backbone element *(gugan fenzi)* of the Gang of Four or committed some serious crime, including participation in counterrevolutionary activity; and (2) that the individual candidate had engaged in lesser criminal activities such as "beating, smashing, and stealing," demonstrating thereby an erroneous political attitude, low political consciousness, or a defective moral character. But candidates can also be disqualified for admission to college if: (3) their parents or others in their sphere of immediate "social relations" fall into the first category of key Gang of Four supporters or perpetrators of serious crimes including counterrevolutionary activity; and (4) the candidates refuse to draw a clear line *(huaqing jiexian)* between themselves and the offenders by openly disavowing the latters' actions. The disavowal must be such that "everyone who knows the person will also know whether he/she has drawn the line clearly."[7]

The daughter of Gang of Four member Zhang Chunqiao was cited as an example of the sort of person who would be prevented from entering college on the latter two grounds, since the young woman is known to have refused to criticize her father. The case is a hypothetical one since Ms. Zhang in fact studied at Fudan University before 1976. But she is among the young "worker-peasant-soldier" teachers who have recently been sent away from the university to work elsewhere allegedly because of their inferior academic qualifications.

Administrators also said that some institutions of higher learning, such as those run by the army or related to national defense, do not admit candidates with serious political/criminal problems in their family histories—even if the candidates do disassociate themselves from the offending relatives' actions.

But this was said to be no longer the case for most civilian institutions, whether keypoint or ordinary.

The administrators were referring to the system of "national security ranks" *(miji)* and by inference to the long-standing practice of channeling students with different kinds of "political liabilities" into different kinds of schools. As we shall see below, some candidates are disqualified altogether on medical grounds while others are restricted in what they study depending on the severity of their health problem. Similarly, candidates are either disqualified for political reasons or given a "conditional pass" depending on the severity of their political handicap.

This practice has always been most strictly applied in defense-related schools and specialties. In addition, from about 1957 onward, it became increasingly difficult for students with even moderately serious political problems to gain admission to keypoint universities, although they could still study at ordinary institutions. Consequently, candidates and earlier college graduates who had such problems were, for example, often assigned to study or work at teachers' training colleges. This not surprisingly contributed further to the unpopularity of those institutions since it turned them into a dumping ground for the politically handicapped.

Despite the administrators' implied assertions that the key universities, as opposed to defense-related institutions, no longer concerned themselves with such political problems, contemporary press reports indicated the contrary. In answering readers' questions as to why some candidates who had met the academic requirements for key schools were not admitted to them, a Shanghai newspaper acknowledged that if candidates had "some problems" in their political assessments, these "could influence admission" to key schools.[8] And a less than perfect political assessment was cited generally, along with serious health problems, as being among the reasons why high-scoring candidates might be passed over during the selection process for their preferred universities, or even fail to gain admission to any college at all.[9]

In 1981, however, the national enrollment regulations announced the abolition of the requirement that the political assessment indicate the candidate's national security rank. Given the comments made by administrators in late 1980 about the continuing national defense concerns, it remains unclear whether these were actually canceled by the abolition order announced in February 1981, or whether the cancellation applies only to the actual rank order system. The latter seems more likely. The official report accompanying this item of the 1981 regulations stated that since the practice of drawing the security ranks on the basis of the candidates' family origins and main social relationships was no longer appropriate for the nation's class situation, the national security ranks would no longer be drawn. But the report continued that the enrollment of new students in secret *(jimi)* and top-secret *(juemi)* specialties would be "decided according to policy and the candidates' actual situations."[10]

No statistics are available concerning either the number of candidates who are denied admission to college for political reasons or the number whose placement in college has been affected by a political assessment which is, as they say, "not clear." In Shanghai and Jiangsu, where the political assessment was being compiled prior to the written examinations, administrators would say only that "a few" or "a very few" candidates were barred from taking the examinations on political grounds each year. Elsewhere, administrators said that "fewer" are disqualified from college for political than for health reasons.

In any case, the universities themselves have no direct knowledge of what has gone wrong for candidates declared ineligible for college admission. Such individuals are either prevented by their middle schools or work units from taking the written examinations or, if the political assessment is conducted after the exams, the names of those found to be ineligible are simply withdrawn from the list of active candidates. The files of these students are not forwarded to the enrollment center, and the university enrollment personnel have no knowledge of their existence.

Reports vary as to whether the candidates themselves have the right to see their own political assessments, and it is possible that the practice itself varies from place to place. All of my sources on this subject agree that prior to 1966, the confidentiality of this document was strictly guarded by the Party organization—specifically, by the Party-controlled personnel cadres of the candidate's middle school or work unit. Students were, however, usually advised informally as to the contents of their political dossiers, which the Red Guards' forays into personnel offices in the late 1960s opened up to public scrutiny for the first time.

To summarize, the candidate's class background and family history officially may no longer be used as criteria for admission to college.[11] For at least twenty years prior to 1978, when the rules were changed, the candidate's family background was the key variable in determining political eligibility for college. Today, educators all assert that the candidate's own political behavior and general character have become the primary criteria. In practice, however, the "internal" realities complicate the simplicity of the publicly proclaimed ideals and regulations. In this case, the principle of family responsibility for the political and criminal behavior of its members has not been completely abandoned, as is attested to by the political qualifications for admission to college described above which were corroborated at five universities.[12]

Nevertheless, the range of family problems for which a candidate may be held politically liable has been significantly reduced and refined. Hence class or occupational designations of family members are presumably no longer being used against college candidates. The chief beneficiaries of this change are the children of capitalists, landlords, and rich peasants—all of whom were previously denied access in some way or other.

Gone, too, are the historical political problems dating back to before Liberation, and most political problems dating from 1949 through 1976. Among the beneficiaries in this category would be the children of "rightists," a designation which was applied mainly to intellectuals deemed hostile to socialism and Party rule. Another group of beneficiaries are young people with "historical counterrevolutionaries" in their families, the designation for persons associated in various ways with the pre-1949 Guomindang regime. Yet another group of beneficiaries are the children of cadres who fell into serious political disfavor sometime after 1949, and especially after 1966.

Indeed, virtually all the social/political categories that were discriminated against through the Cultural Revolution decade have now been exonerated (with the exception of various "radical" elements which were caught up in the twisting currents of Cultural Revolution politics as epitomized by the Lin Biao affair). But the exonerated categories have been replaced by a much smaller array of *current* political/criminal problems as defined by the new post-Mao Admistration. And children of people with such problems are discriminated against. Thus the children of Gang of Four supporters—the operational definition of which appears to vary locally—and those of active counterrevolutionaries as well as convicted criminals are still being denied access to a college education, just as the children of many others were excluded before.

The similarities and differences between the present and the pre-1978 past are reflected clearly in the information required of the candidates on their secondary school graduation and college application forms. The candidates must still declare the key details of their own and their families' political, social, and criminal histories. This information may still be used against them in various ways. It may keep them out of college altogether, or it may keep them from entering certain schools and fields of study. But at the same time, the new definition of family origin for young people today replaces the negative economic and class distinctions originating in the pre-1949 past with the entirely respectable occupations of the post-liberation present. This automatically eliminates the entire category of class distinctions from the list of qualifications for admission to college.

The Physical Examination (shenti jiancha)

Whether scheduled before the written exams or after, the physical examination is conducted in accordance with requirements and standards fixed jointly by the Ministries of Health and Education. There are some ten kinds of serious health problems which can disqualify a candidate for admission to any institution of higher learning. Some of these illnesses are so serious as to physically prevent the individual from participating in regular classroom activity. Others seem to indicate the lower level of medical care available in China since a person suffering from them would be able to attend college with proper treatment. Still others of these health problems appear to reflect differing cultural assumptions concerning the appropriate relationship between physical fitness and academic training or intellectual development. The health problems which can disqualify an individual for admission to college are:

(1) Serious congenital heart disease.
(2) Low blood pressure (90/60 or below) and high blood pressure (140/80 or above).
(3) Active pulmonary tuberculosis.
(4) Chronic hepatitis.
(5) Diabetes.
(6) Acute arthritis.
(7) Serious kidney disease.
(8) Any serious physical handicap or deformity, such as, for example, the muscular atrophy resulting from infantile paralysis or a difference of more than three centimeters in the length of the legs.
(9) Severely defective hearing or eyesight, the latter being defined as the corrected sight of both eyes measuring 0.4 or lower (normal eyesight on this scale ranges from 1.5 to 0.5).
(10) Epilepsy; unspecified "malfunctions of the nervous system"; and unspecified "disabilities due to brain injury."[13]

As an integral part of the enrollment process, the formal medical exam must be given by authorized medical personnel. On the appointed day, the candidates are accompanied to the hospital by their classroom teachers or a responsible person from their work units. The forms containing the results of the physical examinations remain in the keeping of the accompanying person, who is responsible for showing them to the candidates. In order to preclude surreptitious alterations, the candidates themselves are not supposed to keep the completed forms.

The two most common results at this stage are an unconditional pass for candidates in good health or a conditional pass for candidates whose health disqualifies them from entering certain, but not all, fields of study. The physical qualifications for particular courses of study are fixed by the Ministries of Health and Education and are widely publicized, though in so detailed a form as to render it all but impossible for the layman to match the physical qualifications with the particular academic specialties in question. The doctor is responsible for identifying on the medical report any field of study for which the candidate is not qualified; and teachers are responsible for explaining the significance of the limitations to the candidates. This part of the process is not always well coordinated, however. Administrators in Shanghai complained that even there, where communications and facilities are among the best in the country, candidates sometimes disqualify themselves from college altogether because they mistakenly enter on their preference forms only specialties to which they cannot be admitted for health reasons.

The following six representative items, drawn from the much longer list of qualifying conditions, appear to reflect the same mix of underlying assumptions and objective conditions as the more serious illnesses and disabilities listed above:

(1) Candidates at various stages of recovery from bronchial, pulmonary, and extrapulmonary forms of tuberculosis may not be enrolled in a wide variety of fields, including specialties in the fine arts that require the study of vocal music or wind instruments; such engineering subjects as geological prospecting, hydrology, and cartography; forestry; water transport; geography; archaeology; and physical education.

(2) Candidates with severe varicose veins or flat feet will not be enrolled in most specialties requiring field work; physical education; or performing arts specialties. The slightly lame are also ineligible for these courses of study and for those related to foreign affairs and foreign trade as well.

(3) Color-blind candidates and those lacking a sense of smell will not be admitted to specialties which require those sensibilities.

(4) Persons with impaired eyesight are not admitted to a wide variety of specialties, primarily in the sciences and engineering. Differing degrees of impairment are carefully matched with different specialties.

(5) Those with facial abnormalities, including convergent squint (cross-eyed), divergent squint (wall-eyed), harelip, and serious scars or birth marks, will be denied admission to several maritime transport specialties and to all specialties in foreign affairs, foreign trade, the fine arts, and teacher training.

(6) Some specialties, including physical education and all those in teacher training, do not admit candidates who cannot meet certain minimum specifications of height and weight.[14]

In addition to the preenrollment physical all candidates must undergo, most universities give their own follow-up exam once the new students arrive on campus. The purpose is to discover any infectious diseases that may have been contracted in the interim—hepatitis being the single most common problem in this respect—or any errors in the formal physical exam. Those candidates found to be in the former category must take leave of absence pending recovery. Those in the latter will either be denied admission if the problem is serious enough or transferred to another specialty if possible. The "errors" can sometimes be deliberate. Administrators noted that influencing the medical examiners to alter the health report is a form of cheating, or "going through the back door," that candidates do sometimes attempt.

Again, administrators could provide few statistics concerning those disqualified from college for health reasons at any of the stages described above. It was acknowledged only that "more" candidates are disqualified for health than for political reasons and that relatively few problems were discovered during the final follow-up exam. In 1979, for example, Jilin University refused to accept a new freshman with a lame leg. Also in 1979, Lanzhou University sent four new students home for one-year leaves of absence, out of a total freshman class of 1,060. East China Teachers' Training University similarly rejected eight students from a total freshman class of 1,241 in 1980.

According to one press report, the follow-up health exams in 1981 at Zhongshan University, South China Industrial Institute, Zhongshan Medical College, and other schools in Guangzhou uncovered intentional and unintentional errors serious enough to cost seven new students their seats in college. One member of this group, admitted to the geology department at Zhongshan University, was found to be crippled from polio, a fact not recorded on his medical report. Another case was that of an epileptic, newly enrolled in the Chinese language department at the same university, who had successfully hidden the illness until suffering a seizure the second day at school. A third case, this one at the Zhongshan Medical College, involved a new student found to be of substandard size, standing a mere four feet eight inches tall and weighing only sixty-six pounds. An additional fifty-two new students were found to have contracted hepatitis and other infectious diseases and were granted one-year leaves of absence.[15] Other statistics of this nature gleaned from the press are compiled in table 5 (p. 127).

Like the political requirements, the health regulations are applied more rigorously with respect to the keypoint schools than to others during the actual selection process. Thus in 1980, when candidates in Shanghai met the academic requirements of the key universities but were not admitted to them, the reason in most cases was some health problem. Near-sighted and color-blind candidates, along with others having higher than normal blood pressure or a faster than normal heartbeat, were often passed over by key universities which would otherwise have admitted them. And because of the "conditional pass" they received on their physical exams, such candidates often had difficulty gaining admission even to ordinary schools, despite their high examination scores.[16] Similarly, a "less than perfect" *(jiaocha)* health record was cited generally as one reason why a high-scoring candidate might be passed over in the selection process and fail to gain admission to college altogether.[17]

The assumption underlying these restrictions is that since the nation's resources are so scarce, its needs so great, and its college places so few, the state should invest only in those candidates from whom it is likely to receive the greatest return over time. While economists would doubtless applaud so rigorous an application of the value-for-money approach, it stands in sharp contrast to contemporary international standards in education, which generally require a physical exam at the outset of a student's college career but for purposes of treatment rather than exclusion. And indeed, some of the restrictions suggest an arbitrary and unnecessary waste of talent. The 1983 enrollment regulations belatedly acknowledged this fact, authorizing the provincial enrollment committees to make exceptions for candidates who are physically handicapped but "especially outstanding" *(tebie youxiu)* academically. Whether there is to be a more general revision in the principle and practice of exclusion based on health grounds remains to be seen. The 1983 regulations suggest that the exception is intended only for the few truly exceptional individuals who have been able to surmount and circumvent the restrictions that have also been placed on their admission to keypoint secondary schools.

Chinese educators explained informally that the regulations preventing those with facial irregularities from studying subjects which will bring them into contact with foreigners reflect China's sensitivity about its image vis-à-vis the outside world. Ironically, the "sensitivity" in this case appears to be superficial at best, since much of the outside world assumes such values to have been dead for several decades, at least insofar as matters of state policy are concerned. That they are not is demonstrated by China's fascination with eugenics, which has gained new respectability in recent years. It is now officially promoted, inspiring suggestions in the press that idiots and the seriously deformed be put down at birth; that care be taken "not to fall in love with sick people who should not marry"; and that those with "hereditary diseases" be "dissuaded" from marrying and reproducing themselves.[18] The application of eugenics is now lauded as a "long-term strategic task to cope with China's four modernizations."[19]

Policy and practice with respect to the physical requirements for admission to college appear to reflect this preoccupation with physical superiority as much as they do the economics of scarcity or the relatively unsophisticated nature of health care generally available in China at the present time. The trend, moreover, is in the direction of a more rigorous application of the same principles. Mindful of the large number of candidates barred by the health regulations from various fields of study, the Education Ministry stipulated in 1981 that when qualifications are otherwise similar, candidates who have achieved the national physical fitness standards *(guojia tiyu duanlian biaozhun)* should be given preference in admission to college. The eventual objective stated then was that all candidates be able to achieve these standards as a prerequisite for admission to college.[20]

The national physical fitness standards include specific requirements for men and women in a variety of tests, including long- and short-distance running, high and broad jumping, push-ups, throwing (dummy hand grenades and shots), carrying weights, and marching.[21] At this juncture, the outside observer cannot but wonder why the Ministries of Health and Education do not bestir themselves to promote similarly rigorous national standards for sanitation and nutrition. However great progress has been in these areas over the past thirty years, it now appears to have leveled off at a plane well below the accepted world standards to which China generally aspires. The productivity of China's college students would surely be better served by greater attention to these two most basic causes of the nation's collective poor health, so frequently lamented in the Chinese press, than by setting mechanical requirements for running and jumping as prerequisites for admission to college. At a minimum, certainly, the waste of student manpower created by the widely prevalent diseases of hepatitis and tuberculosis could be significantly reduced by greater efforts in this area.

The Preference Form (zhiyuanbiao)

The step that can turn all of the above plans and preparations into a game of chance for the candidate is the writing of the preference form. Each candidate is permitted to list five key and five non-key institutions in order of preference. Some provinces allow candidates to write an additional short list of preferences for the specialized junior colleges, which offer two- or three-year courses of study (referred to as *gaodeng zhuanke*, or *dazhuan;* the regular four- or five-year courses of study are called *benke).*

Each candidate may also indicate two preferred academic departments or major fields of study at each university listed and in any combination. The only restriction is that those taking the liberal arts section of the written examinations may not apply to major in science specialties and vice versa.

Prior to 1980, candidates usually filled in only the major field of study, or specialty *(zhuanye),* as it is commonly called. In recognition of the fact that students may not be knowledgeable enough to make so specific and narrow a choice at the start of their college careers, the rules were changed in 1980 to encourage the writing of preferred academic departments only on the application form.[22] According to university administrators, this move was part of a reform aimed at discouraging students from specializing until sometime after the completion of their freshman year. This reform has apparently been inspired by foreign, or at least American, criticism of overspecialization within the Chinese system of higher education—which is, in this respect, still based upon the model introduced from the Soviet Union in the early 1950s. The Chinese mention this criticism. They are aware that in American universities, the first two years of college are usually devoted to general course work and the student does not really begin specializing until the junior year. Precisely how this reform is to be implemented in China remains unclear, given the very specific nature of the national enrollment plan. However, by 1981 several universities were announcing their individual enrollment plans by department rather than by specialty.[23]

Candidates are also asked to indicate on the preference form their willingness to accept arbitrary assignment if they cannot be admitted to their preferred schools. If they do not so indicate, they are considered for enrollment only at those schools and in the departments or specialties that they have listed on their preference forms. Candidates who indicate their willingness to accept arbitrary assignment but then refuse to do so are, like those who refuse to accept assignment at a school they have listed, barred from taking the examinations the following year. As noted, the ban applies for only one year.

The use of the preference form in this fashion dates back to the 1950s, when it was devised to solve the problems resulting from the introduction of unified planned enrollment. Initially, this entailed the arbitrary assignment of candidates to schools and courses of study. During the Cultural Revolution decade, however, the candidate's preference was not given such consideration. At that time, the specific enrollment plans for both universities and majors were handed down from province to city or county, and on down to the individual work units, whether communes, factories, or enterprises. These, as noted, were responsible for nominating candidates to fill a specific place in a given university and specialty. Under this system, mismatching between the interests of the candidates and the subjects they were assigned to study was said to be common.

With the restoration of the preference procedure, this problem is, by all accounts, much improved today. Nevertheless, the candidate approaches this step with some trepidation, since an inappropriate listing of preferences may result in a failure to be admitted altogether, despite a satisfactory score on the written examinations. Yet the universities themselves are often left with unfilled quotas, as will be seen below.

The exercise is complicated because it represents not just the candidates' own preferences but also their calculation of the schools and specialties to which they have the most realistic chance of being admitted. To make such a decision, candidates ideally need to know: (1) how well they have done on the examinations *relative* to everyone else; (2) how many places have been allotted to their particular province in any given specialty or department at any given school; and (3) how many other candidates have applied in those same specialties, since the greater the competition, the higher a candidate will have to score in order to succeed. The more information the candidates have on each of these points at the time they file the preference form, the less of a gamble their choices represent.

It is left to the provinces, however, to decide how much of this information to provide their candidates, and there is considerable variation in this area. At one extreme are Shanghai and Beijing, which now require that the preference form be filled out prior to the written examinations when no information on performance is available. Moreover, although the enrollment announcements in the press for both cities in 1980 and 1981 listed the schools and departments or specialties that have admissions quotas in those two cities, the size of these quotas was omitted. Hence, the candidates did not know precisely how many seats they were competing for unless this information was conveyed to them by some other means.[24]

At the other extreme is Zhejiang province, where the 1981 candidates did not write the preference form until *after* the publication in the provincial press of: (1) the specific number of Zhejiang students to be admitted into each department or specialty in each institution enrolling them throughout the country; (2) the candidates had been notified of their own individual examination scores; and (3) the announcement of the minimum passing scores for Zhejiang candidates in regular *(benke)*, non-keypoint universities (liberal arts, 393 points; science and engineering, 422 points; foreign languages, 330 points, or 325 points total if the single foreign language exam score was 90 points or higher); and the same breakdown of separate mps for the specialized junior college *(zhuanke)* courses.[25]

Yet another variation was found in Guangdong province, where the preference forms in 1980 were written *after* the candidates had been informed of both their own scores and whether they had passed the provincial mps, but *before* the mps itself was publicly announced. The candidates therefore had no sense of their performance relative to that of everyone else, as was true in Shandong in 1980 as well.[26]

Candidates in Jiangsu province in 1980 wrote the preference *after* the mps had been announced. This was changed in 1981 to require candidates to write their preferences immediately after the examinations, but *before* they had been corrected or any scores announced. The city of Tianjin also followed this latter procedure in 1981.[27]

Thus, candidates must often write their preferences "somewhat blindly," as some administrators noted, although more so in some provinces than in others. Where the candidates do not have open access to the full range of possible information, it is the responsibility of teachers and local enrollment offices to provide assistance. In Guangdong, even though the provincial enrollment quota breakdown by college and specialty was not printed in the newspapers, these figures were announced by the local enrollment offices, and "all middle schools and their students came to know of this announcement." The graduating seniors are supposed to be advised by their teachers as to which colleges and specialties will have more places available than others. Also, certain patterns from previous years are well known, and this information is passed on to the candidates. For example, Guangxi province has traditionally sent relatively large quotas of students to Guangdong schools each year, and this can be expected to continue.[28]

That certain specialties are unpopular, or "cold" *(lengmen)*, and their quotas regularly undersubscribed is also well known. University administrators identified these subjects readily, and they are listed above in the Introduction. Candidates with only average academic records are always advised to keep such fields of study in mind when filling out their preference forms and to avoid the popular *(remen)* specialties with potentially "glorious" *(guangrong)* futures which attract large numbers of applicants. More generally, candidates are said to favor the sciences; to lack interest in the liberal arts, education, engineering, and agronomy; and to "be afraid of" philosophy and politics.[29]

It is the responsibility of their teachers to advise the candidates concerning the specialties for which they are most likely to qualify, given their abilities, interests, and the nature of the anticipated competition. Such tips were once part of the "technical advice" for filling out the preference forms that was passed on from year to year before the Cultural Revolution by teachers, parents, elder siblings, and local enrollment offices. This game-plan approach to college admissions subsequently came in for much criticism by student Red Guards. But the custom has now been fully revived.

One municipal enrollment office in Jiangsu province, seeking to alleviate anxieties generated by the new procedure in 1981 (the switch to writing the preference form before the scores were announced), offered suggestions to "energetically overcome blindness" in filling out the preference form. Candidates were advised, among other things, to consider their general past academic record as well as their comparative performance in different subjects, and to pay attention to the numbers thought to be enrolling in different schools.[30]

The Tianjin enrollment office did the same, reminding candidates that although they could write a total of ten different schools and twenty specialties, the first listed was always the most important and should therefore be most carefully considered. This is because the timing and mechanics of the selection process are such that only the first two or three choices can usually be given proper consideration by the universities' enrollment personnel. Average students should therefore take care not to write Beijing or Qinghua Universities as their first choice since they would not qualify at either. Meanwhile, the quotas of their less favored schools would have already been filled with those schools' own first-choice candidates, leaving little room for third- or fourth-preference candidates. Candidates who make this kind of miscalculation can lose out altogether and not gain admission to any university.

Another key principle is to rank the preferences *in descending order*, not with reference to the candidate's own choices, but with respect to the quality of the schools. A candidate who does not score high enough for Beijing University is not likely to score high enough for Qinghua or the Chinese University of Science and Technology (Hefei) either. Candidates are therefore advised not to list more than one top-ranking school and always to list the others in descending order based on their reputed entrance standards.[31]

The minimum passing scores of individual schools are never announced in advance, but this information circulates among educators based on the records of earlier years. Candidates are also cautioned to pay attention to the available materials that indicate specific requirements for different institutions and specialties, e.g., whether they enroll women, whether their foreign-language requirement is especially rigorous, the particular physical prerequisites, and so forth.[32]

The universities themselves are playing an increasingly important role in this activity as part of their drive for more autonomy with respect to recruiting. The standard practice is for each institution to print up and send out brochures and posters to the localities where they have been assigned enrollment quotas. These advertisements introduce the universities and their fields of study in very general terms to the graduating seniors and are circulated among the middle schools for that purpose. Zhongshan University said it sends out several thousands of these advertisements each year. Universities also do some recruiting on their own, often sending their materials directly to the best key middle schools in an effort to encourage the best students to apply to their institutions.

More significant—and not yet publicly acknowledged—are all of the practices associated with the special links that are being established *(guagou)* between key universities and key middle schools. This was criticized during the Cultural Revolution as an elitist measure that gave unfair advantage to students in a very few schools. But this practice, too, is now being resumed. Universities in Shanghai and Guangzhou had already begun to establish such links as of 1980, and others elsewhere were planning to follow suit. Fudan University, for example, had established such relationships with ten of the best middle schools in Shanghai. Fudan directs special attention toward these schools, sending, along with the posters and propaganda materials, university personnel to talk to the seniors, who are also invited to the Fudan campus to see the laboratories and other facilities. And, indeed, the main purpose of the relationship is to ensure that the teachers in these schools follow up the university's recruiting efforts by encouraging the best students to make Fudan their first choice. In return, Fudan guarantees such students priority in admission over others of similar qualifications. It is this latter trade-off that has not yet been publicized, presumably due to the connotations of unfair advantage it entails. Fudan also offers short refresher courses for the teachers of these middle schools. The purpose is both to improve the quality of their teaching and to help the schools coordinate more closely with the demands of the university curricula.[33]

For those not fortunate enough to attend such well-connected middle schools, or for those with less than brilliant academic records, the standing advice is to indicate on the preference form their willingness to accept arbitrary assignment—which, for some universities, is the only way to fill their quotas for unpopular subjects. Such students are also encouraged to include among their preferences some of the ever increasing number of tertiary-level technical courses, junior colleges, and vocational universities.

Nevertheless, a perfect match between preferences, performance, and the specific enrollment quotas is impossible to achieve. In 1981 the city of Guangzhou acknowledged the problem of relatively high-scoring candidates being eliminated from the competition due to their unrealistic preferences by formally allowing them to modify these choices after the keypoint universities had completed their selection. More than three hundred Guangzhou candidates who achieved scores high enough to qualify for admission to keypoint universities that year were not admitted to any of them. Guangdong's total provincial quota for key or first-category universities in 1981 was something over four thousand. The city enrollment office therefore decided to allow the three hundred candidates in Guangzhou to amend their preference forms—encouraging them to indicate a willingness to accept arbitrary assignment—before the selection for ordinary or second-category institutions commenced.[34]

Yet even some key universities have difficulty filling their quotas in unpopular subjects. Educators all described the phenomenon in similar terms while refusing to speculate on the underlying causes. Candidates are, on the whole, unwilling to venture very far beyond their own provinces. They tend to concentrate their preferences in a few popular specialties, in a few of the most famous institutions, and as close to home as possible. This is especially true if home is a big city, in which case an ordinary local institution may actually be more attractive to local youth than nearby national key schools. This is not only because the admissions standards at the former are somewhat lower. It is also because there will be guaranteed local employment after graduation instead of the uncertainty inherent in a job assignment under the national unified plan which governs the futures of graduates from the national key schools.

So great was the competition for places at one such school, Beijing Teachers' Training College *(xueyuan)*, that its mps in the late 1970s was reportedly pushed up to a level not far behind the leading schools in the city, an unprecedented occurrence for such an institution. Similar competition for places at Shanghai's municipal colleges led to rumors in 1981 that their graduates might be required to accept job assignments outside the city. Thus the kind of job assignment that can be anticipated after graduation is also an important factor in determining the candidate's academic preferences.

Candidates also appear to have an innate distaste for the rigors of "field work" and therefore tend to avoid those specialties which will oblige them to venture into such inhospitable physical environments as mountains, deserts, oceans, and mines. This accounts for the perennial difficulty of filling the freshman quotas in geology, geography, and petroleum engineering, to name a few. Students today are said to prefer not just those specialties promising a "glorious" future but also one that is safe, secure, and close to home. And now that there are no political costs or benefits associated with saying no, many are unwilling to accept arbitrary assignment.

The subheadings in a composite of testimonials aimed at the 1981 Shanghai candidates and written by Shanghai college students with undesirable school assignments reflect prevailing attitudes but probably did little to change them: "Dedicating one's life *(xianshen)* to the fatherland through the study of oceanography"; "There is joy in the bitterness of studying geology"; and "Shanghai students most certainly can adapt to life elsewhere."[35] Gone are the days, it was said, when Shanghai teenagers volunteered by the thousands, as they did in the late 1950s and early 1960s, to participate in projects such as the work-study agricultural school in Jiangxi which they built into the famous Communist Labor University. Lauded then by all the nation's top leaders, such tasks were held up as "glorious" for the young people of the time.

Even more striking are the contrasts between today's youth and the generations who grew up in the 1930s and 1940s. One university vice-president recalled that she had run away from a comfortable home at the age of fourteen to join the guerrillas and fight the Japanese. A few middle-aged and elderly administrators lamented the passing of that enthusiasm for the revolution and for the work of national reconstruction as they recalled nostalgically the idealism and activities of their own youth. There were still tough jobs to be done, they noted, but young people appeared to have lost interest in the challenge. The nation's leaders now praise other heroes, and the values of young people have changed with them.

Administrators commented in particular on the new "homing instinct" of Chinese youth who, unlike their counterparts of earlier years, are often reluctant even to apply to universities outside their home provinces, much less look forward to job assignment there. Though lacking any explanation for this phenomenon, administrators asserted that it is much more pronounced at present than it ever was before the Cultural Revolution. They do not recall a time when it was as difficult to assign young people to out-of-province colleges.

This trend may be reinforced, so far as college application is concerned, by the pattern of enrollment quotas, which are now known to be substantially larger for local than for out-of-province students. Or the quota patterns may themselves simply reflect this trend, which became apparent immediately after the college entrance examinations were restored. For example, in 1980 the

Tianjin Enrollment Committee issued a special plea urging candidates to apply to outside universities in order to prevent a recurrence of a problem that first appeared in 1979. That year, outside universities were assigned to enroll 1,767 students from Tianjin but fell short by 388. Those failing to fill their quotas in Tianjin included forty key institutions. Tianjin's quotas the following year reflected this shortfall, with only 1,320 students planned for outside enrollment. The city's total college enrollment quota in 1980 was 5,400, including those to be sent to colleges outside Tianjin.[36]

One additional bias that influences the college application process is the desire to avoid schools and specialties that "face the countryside." Those that are likely to lead to a job assignment in the rural areas are not popular. Medical college applications plummeted in one province in 1982, following the circulation of a rumor that all 1982 freshmen would be assigned upon graduation to rural commune-level hospitals.

In response to this problem, the Ministry of Education began promoting a new scheme in 1983 called "directional enrollment and job assignment" *(dingxiang zhaosheng, dingxiang fenpei)*, to be carried out mainly by provincial agricultural, forestry, medical, and teacher training colleges. The new method cannot make these schools any more popular; but it will, if implemented, at least ensure that the graduates of these institutions accept rural job assignments. It is based on the assumption that only students from the rural areas can be recruited into such schools and now they must also promise, in the manner of a contract agreement, to accept the rural job assignment after graduation. There will be penalties if the promise is not honored. The schools are, in return, authorized to lower their admissions standards for candidates willing to enter into this agreement.[37]

The scheme bears a certain unheralded resemblance to the "from the commune, to the commune" *(shelai shequ)* principle of enrollment/job assignment promoted before 1976. Apparently, very few college students were actually enrolled in accordance with that principle in the early 1970s. But it was neverthelss advertised as one of the "glorious" innovations of the period designed to benefit peasants and urban youth working in the communes. By contrast, directional enrollment is without pretense and it drives a hard bargain—for rural youth only.

Finally, sex stereotyping appears to be accepted by men and women alike without question. Women are said to prefer the fields of foreign languages, medicine, and teacher training and to apply in greater numbers for them as a result. Those who apply in the sciences prefer subjects that require "careful and fine work" such as analytic chemistry for which they have an instinctive aptitude. The study and work associated with specialties performed entirely in the laboratory are, in any case, "more appropriate" for women than such physically arduous subjects as geology, geography, and even archaeology, which require extensive work "in the field." Concern about the inability of women in particular to sustain the physical hardships associated with field work was expressed repeatedly as the main reason for their small to nonexistent presence in such specialties. Also regularly cited was the unquestioning assumption that since everyone wants to have children and since women are responsible for rearing them, women especially most choose fields of study that will permit them simultaneously to work and remain close to hearth and home. Educators everywhere, both male and female, simply laughed at the notion that fathers and mothers might be equally responsible for the task of raising children.

CHAPTER IV

The Examinations: Administering, Correcting, And Determining the Minimum Passing Score

The examinations are given each year on three consecutive days in July. Since all of China is on the same time standard, the exams are administered in the same sequence and at the same time across the country. At least one central location per county is designated as a testing site, with middle school and college classrooms serving as the examination halls *(kaochang)*. Between twenty-five and thirty candidates are normally seated in a single room. Since the desks in most Chinese classrooms are arranged in adjoining pairs, only one candidate is permitted to occupy each pair of desks during the exams, a precaution against cheating.

Each examination is two hours in length, with the exceptions of Chinese language, a two-and-one-half-hour exam, and biology, introduced as a forty-five-minute exam in 1981. A total of nine subjects are now covered by the examinations. All science and engineering candidates must take exams in: politics, Chinese language, mathematics, chemistry, physics, biology, and a foreign language. Those opting for the liberal arts track must be examined in: politics, Chinese language, mathematics, history, geography, and a foreign language. Science and liberal arts candidates now take different math exams. Moreover, on the Chinese language exam, the two groups do not have to answer all of the same questions, and correction standards are applied more rigorously for liberal arts candidates than for those in the sciences.

The choice of one of six foreign language exams is left up to the candidate. Most select English, Russian, or Japanese. The other three possibilities are French, Spanish, and German. In 1980 the foreign-language exam was weighted at only 30 percent of the grade earned, and in 1981 at 50 percent (that is, a perfect score of 100 points would earn only 50 points). Similarly, biology in 1981 was weighted at only 30 percent of the grade earned. This partial weighting was adopted since many middle schools were still unable to teach foreign languages and biology in the late 1970s. By 1983, 50 percent weight was being given to biology and full weight to the foreign language exam. But the individual provinces were authorized to decide whether or not their junior colleges had to take the foreign language exam for full credit or "for reference" only.

The written foreign language exam for those seeking to major in foreign languages has always been fully credited, however, while their math exam was until 1983 used only for reference. An oral examination in their chosen language is evaluated separately.[1]

Thus, based on a perfect score of 100 points per subject, the maximum total score possible per candidate in 1980 was 500 points for foreign language majors and 530 points for all others. In 1981 the maximum score possible was again 500 points for foreign-language candidates, 550 points for other liberal arts candidates, and 580 points for science candidates.

These totals do not include the more difficult supplementary questions for which additional points were granted for the first time in 1981. The supplementary questions on that year's exams were worth an additional 20 points on the math exam for science candidates and 10 points on the Chinese language exam for liberal arts candidates, reflecting the effort to place greater weight on those two basic subjects. If the value of these supplementary questions is included, the maximum scores possible in 1981 were actually 510 points for foreign language candidates, 560 points for those in liberal arts, and 600 points for science candidates.[2]

The written examinations are now compulsory for all college candidates. In 1977 the Ministry of Education stipulated that a few students with some special talent or accomplishment could be admitted to college without taking the written exams. Under this regulation, the Chinese language department at Shandong University admitted in 1977 a thirty-eight year-old peasant who had already written and published a number of works. In 1978 and 1979 there were widely publicized national and provincial competitions in math, physics, and chemistry, and the winners were admitted to college without having to sit for the written college entrance examinations. These two forms of exemption permitted between 1977 and 1979 have now been eliminated.

The universities themselves are also authorized to give a "retest" *(fucha)* to newly admitted students. Most, though not all, of the universities visited reported giving the new arrivals some kind of written test shortly after the start of the autumn semester. Though the formal objective of this procedure is to ensure that no unworthy candidate has slipped through the net, the universities indicated that this testing is essentially a formality; some referred to it as a kind of placement test. Only one university, Wuhan, reported new students failing this test, which usually covers only one or two subjects. At Wuhan, about forty of the nine hundred freshmen in 1979 failed this test and were required to take it again. All but two passed the second time, but these two were allowed to remain in school pending improvement of their performance which did occur in both cases. The national entrance examinations thus remain the principal criterion for admission to college.

Producing the Examination Questions

Elaborate precautions are taken to ensure secrecy and fairness at all stages of the examination process. The work of writing the exam questions is organized by the Education Ministry, which invites different teachers to participate each year. They are drawn from middle schools, universities, and sometimes also the local education institutes *(jiaoyu xueyuan)*. The latter are long-standing institutions which essentially have three functions: education research, teaching material compilation, and in-service training for middle school teachers. They have no other students and exist in one form or another at all levels, province, city, city-district, and county.

Small groups of teachers (ten or less) write the questions for each subject exam. Prepared with the examination questions are the prescribed answers, together with the maximum number of points to be allotted for each question, the breakdown of points to be allotted each part of a question, and the standards to be used in determining acceptable answers. At the same time, a set of back-up questions and answers is prepared for use in the event of leaks or other contingencies. For example, in 1980 twenty-six examination papers were found to contain blank pages in Zhejiang, and the candidates affected were permitted to retake the examinations concerned using the back-up questions.[3]

In addition, great efforts are made to prevent disclosure of the examination questions and to preserve the anonymity of the teachers responsible for writing them. The anonymity is necessary, it is said, to safeguard against possible reprisals. In 1979, for instance, the chemistry exam contained a number of surprises which could not have been anticipated on the basis of the 1979 review outline. The consternation felt by many candidates and parents over the ensuing low scores was naturally directed against those who had prepared the questions. Promises have since been made that there will be no such surprises in the future. The national secondary school curriculum, completely reunified as of 1981, is supposed to serve as the sole basis for the college entrance exam questions, and the proportion of middle school teachers participating in the preparation of questions is said to have been increased.

A number of measures have been instituted to help maintain the secrecy of this process. First, any teacher who has a relative taking the examinations that year is forbidden to participate in preparing the questions. Second, all of the teachers involved are gathered together in isolated and unspecified resort hotels at different locations each year. While there, the teachers remain incommunicado: no mail, telephone calls, or visitors, not only for the ten days necessary to write the questions but from then until the examinations have been given. These teachers thus enjoy one month or more of contemplation, entertainment, and good food—"partly like being on holiday and partly like being in jail"—all at state expense.

Once the contents have been determined, the examinations are delivered under strictest secrecy to each province and the three autonomous cities, which are individually responsible for printing the number of copies to be distributed in their areas. The provincial printers, like the teachers, are then held incommunicado until the examinations are given. The seals on the envelopes containing the examination papers may not be broken until precisely thirty minutes prior to the start of each exam.[4] After the exams have been graded, however, the questions become public property, and street-corner editions appear within weeks after the scores have been announced. Official editions are subsequently published as review materials for future examinations.[5]

Correcting the Examinations

The task of correcting the exams is organized by the provincial enrollment committees and their offices and has now been unified on an all-province basis. During the first few years after the restoration of the entrance examinations, correction was organized by the prefectures. To oversee this stage of the process, each year the provincial enrollment committees form provincial correction committees *(pingjuan weiyuanhui).* The latter are composed of from ten to twenty leading university cadres and professors whose major function apparently is to lend their authority to the proceedings, since these tend to be accompanied by a good deal of public anxiety over fairness and accuracy. The provincial enrollment offices are responsible for recruiting sufficient numbers of university and senior middle school teachers for the actual grading work. These offices must in addition provide the logistical support necessary to gather the graders together at a few sites in one city for the ten to fourteen days immediately following the examinations during which all correcting work must be completed.

An impressive number of teachers are mobilized for this work each year. In 1980, 3,400 teachers in Shanghai corrected some 720,000 examination papers for the 120,000 candidates who took the college entrance exams and those for the professional secondary schools *(zhongzhuan).* These two sets of exams were being combined and corrected together in many provinces at this time. Beijing similarly reported 3,400 graders for the exams of roughly 100,000 candidates, whereas Tianjin tapped some 2,200 graders for the exams of its 94,000 candidates.[6] When the correction of the exams was being coordinated by the prefectures, most of those participating were middle school teachers. But with the decline in the number of candidates and the centralization of the correction work at the provincial level, college teachers—particularly lecturers—are assuming an increasing share of the burden. Middle school teachers who participate in this process are supposed to be college graduates.

The organization of the actual correction work is even more impressive. Despite marginal variations from one province to another, the correction work is done in essentially the same manner everywhere. It is performed by an array of groups and subgroups which form and reform themselves as the work unfolds.

At the apex of the structure in each province are the leading groups formed for each examination subject. College teachers are responsible for the leadership work. For example, Shandong University's Chinese department was assigned responsibility in 1980 for leading the correction of the Chinese language exam for that province. The members of each leading subject group first meet together to study the exam question, the prescribed answers, and to establish a uniform understanding of the standards to be applied in scoring. These leaders are then responsible for conveying this information downwards to the graders. These are organized initially into large "question groups." There is one such group for each question on each subject examination. Each grader is assigned to a group according to the exam question he/she is assigned to correct. Each grader usually corrects only one question, and all those correcting the same question must first come to a uniform understanding of the standards to be applied.

The actual work of correction, however, is performed by the graders subdivided into small work groups of about ten each. These basic work groups are supposed to be organized so that each includes both university and middle school teachers as well as teachers from different districts and counties. The correction work, which was still being done entirely by hand in the early 1980s, follows everywhere a similar pattern of meticulous checking and rechecking. According to the basic pattern, one small work group is responsible for correcting only one exam question, and this holds true everywhere. Similarly, each teacher usually corrects only one question; and each question is corrected at the first reading by only one teacher. The exceptions are the lengthier essay-type questions in politics and Chinese which are corrected at first reading by two people.

The small work groups are generally organized to work as a team, each team consisting of a sufficient number of groups to answer every question on any given exam subject. Each team is responsible for grading the exam papers in that subject for several classrooms of candidates, each of which contain from twenty-five to thirty people. This practice of correcting the exam papers from each classroom or examination hall together necessitates the careful composition of teachers in the small groups, so as to prevent a concentration of teachers from any particular district being responsible for the papers of candidates from that same district.

After the first reading, the process is repeated at least once. This step varies somewhat from place to place, but in most provinces different groups check the first reading and revise the grade points allocated if necessary. Each question is thus read and evaluated by at least two different examiners and often by several more as well, particularly when disagreements arise. Changes in the allocation of points at this stage are common and are often made in an upward direction. Objective fairness is not the only consideration at work as the examiners revise scores since everyone has their eyes on the minimum passing scores and the provincial rank order that is the end result of the process. Thus the final grades can reflect a certain degree of "provincial chauvinism." A similar "prefectural chauvinism" was discovered to have resulted in significantly different scores between prefectures within the same province when this work was organized at that level. Finally, after the small groups have completed this step, random checks of the same questions corrected by a number of different groups are carried out by members of the leading groups to ascertain that uniform standards have been applied.

The task of adding up the number of points on each exam is also done twice, with a second group checking the totals of the first. And the actual recording of the grade is done twice as well, with one group recording in red ink and the other in black. A group leader is then responsible for verifying that the two are identical.

According to standardized procedure, each candidate is assigned an examination permit number which is written on his/her examination papers. This number, together with any other identifying marks on the papers (e.g., the candidate's name, the name or code number of the candidate's district or county enrollment office, and the number of the candidate's examination hall), are now all supposed to be covered throughout the correction process.

At the end of this painstaking review, the examination papers and scores are sent to the grade recording section of the provincial enrollment office, where each candidate's exam papers are put together. The total score for each candidate is then compiled and recorded and the various minimum passing scores computed. An increasing number of provinces are now supplementing their abacuses and calculators with computers for this final stage of the work, which must be completed by the end of July.[7]

Once the computations have been made and the mps determined, the individual scores are not publicly announced but are sent directly to each candidate via the local enrollment office and sponsoring unit. This represents an improvement over pre-1966 practice, when successful candidates were, in due course, notified of the universities to which they had been admitted but never informed of their individual scores. This allowed maximum leeway for the political manipulations known to have occurred in those years both officially as a matter of state policy and unofficially by those in a position to invoke special privileges for their offspring.

In 1978 and 1979, moreover, candidates who had some doubt about their examination scores could even request a recheck. The privilege of this innovation was widely invoked and errors often discovered. But the practice was abolished in 1980, on grounds that it added too much to the burdens of enrollment work and also because some candidates abused the privilege in an effort to change their exam scores.[8] Many newspaper accounts of the correction process cited here were published to help allay fears about accuracy and uniformity of standards following this cancellation of the candidate's right to request a recheck.

The elaborate precautions against cheating together with the actions that make them necessary spring from the same source, namely, the ancient Chinese custom of trying to beat the system. Everyone has stories of "irregularities" today, comparable to those about the degree candidates of old who sat for the imperial examinations with crib notes written on their sleeves. Each year the press contains many reports of cheating and of the punishments meted out for the perpetrators, which can include job demotion and expulsion from the Communist Party. But the teachers interviewed in Hong Kong report that many cases go undiscovered. At this stage of the enrollment process it is apparently easiest to avoid detection in rural examination centers where everyone knows and protects everyone else.

For example, a county education bureau chief might arrange for a certain teacher to proctor the exams in the hall where his child will be sitting. Or, in issuing the local regulations, he might decree that candidates can leave the hall and go to the toilet unescorted. Both situations would provide candidates with an opportunity to consult carefully concealed crib notes.

Or the candidates might deliberately compose their Chinese language essays in such a way that the teachers correcting them could not help but recognize the writers. The style of a candidate's calligraphy is another give-away. But these two tactics were more effective when the exams were corrected only within each prefecture. Now, the chances of this kind of recognition are minimal. More dangerous because of the likelihood of detection is the attempt to tamper with the exam papers at some point after they have been written.

These practices are no less "irregular," however, than the above-mentioned upward bias that can occur during the grading process itself. Although the authorities are aware of this problem, it has never been singled out for public censure. Yet is is said to be facilitated by surreptitious communications and "intelligence" from other correction centers as the grading work progresses and the various provincial score "returns" begin to come in. The extent to which any of these efforts actually influence enrollments is, of course, impossible to estimate. But since a single point can place a marginal candidate within the score range which would make admission possible, the incentives are great to push up score points by fair means and foul.

Determining the Minimum Passing Score (zuidi luqu fenshuxian)

As has been explained above, the mps is actually a statement of the relationship between the quota of college freshmen and the top scores achieved. Since the quotas are so specific in terms of specialties and schools, this formula can be used to calculate the mps of an individual university, of any specialty within a university, of any given geographic unit, and for any number of different combinations of all these. Hence there can be an overall mps for every province, one for different fields of study, and one for each individual school, to name the most common. Until 1981 there was also a national unified mps for the key universities. The various mps have been used both as publicly announced fixed standards for enrollment and as internal adjustable guidelines. If the trend already apparent in 1980 continues, the mps will shift increasingly from the former to the latter role, as the provincial colleges follow the way of the key institutions in fixing their own individual standards.

Between 1977 and 1980, however, the most significant mps from the candidate's point of view was—and in many provinces still is—the provincial mps. Naturally, this score varies from year to year and from province to province depending on the size of the provincial quota for new students and the examination scores of the candidates. Each provincial mps is broken down into *at least* three separate figures reflecting the different maximum number of points possible in the three main categories of study: science and engineering; liberal arts in general; and foreign languages. There are now also separate, lower scores for the specialized junior college courses.

By 1981, some provinces, among them Jiangsu and Guangdong, were calculating the all-province mps only for ordinary colleges and universities, leaving it to the various cities and prefectures to draw their own, lower mps for the junior colleges enrolling within their boundaries. Available press reports show the range of mps being drawn in 1981. A selection of these are given in table 6 (p. 128).

These provincial and local mps represent the absolute bottom line: candidates scoring below these levels are automatically eliminated from the competition for admission to college. In provinces where the health exam is conducted after the written exams, the provincial mps are commonly referred to as the *tijianxian*, or "physical exam line," indicating that only those who score above that line are eligible to take the physical and thus advance in the enrollment process.

In principle, all out-of-province students are supposed to be enrolled in accordance with the mps of their home provinces and not the mps of the province in which their college is located. In practice, as will be explained more fully below, the principle was by 1980 already being eroded by the demands of individual universities to set their own standards for admission.

The provincial mps is determined by the total enrollment quota for the province, including those who will be assigned to key universities, to all universities outside the province, and to those within it as well. Each province's mps line is drawn solely on the basis of its own enrollment quota, which represents the numbers of its own sons and daughters to be enrolled. This will not be the same as the total number of students to be enrolled in colleges within the province since out-of-province students are not included in this calculation. Hence candidates are supposed to be enrolled in colleges throughout the country on the basis of the standards obtaining in their home provinces.

To this total provincial quota figure is then added a "margin" *(xuanze yudi)* usually ranging from 15-20 percent of the quota. For every place in college, between 1.15 and 1.20 candidates will be allowed to "pass" the written exams. If a province's total quota is 10,000 and a 20 percent margin is used, all those scoring beneath the lowest grade achieved by the top 12,000 candidates are considered to have failed the written examinations. This margin may, however, vary slightly (even within a single province) for the different fields of study. The variation will depend on how high the scores are in relation to the number of seats to be filled. Lower scores—such as those generally achieved in 1979 by science candidates—will necessitate a somewhat larger margin. In 1980, for example, Zhejiang province used a 15 percent margin when drawing the mps in science and liberal arts, but one of 20 percent for the foreign language mps.[9]

The Controversy over the Margin

The provinces themselves have the right to decide precisely how great the margin should be, and in 1980 most provinces claimed to be using 15-20 percent margins.[10] Only Tianjin's margin, reportedly in the 5-10 percent range, fell below the apparent norm.[11]

By contrast, the margins used between 1977 and 1979 tended to be much higher. According to one source, they were as high as 1:2.5 in the late 1970s.[12] Others referred to more modest ratios of 1:1.5 for those years.[13] But because allowing so many more students to pass the written exams than there were places in college "gave too much hope to too many," the large margins have been cut to more realistic levels. The intensity of the emotions aroused by such shattered hopes was brought home to the authorities when Beijing candidates who had achieved the mps but failed to gain admission to college took their protests to the streets in 1979.[14]

When the health and political exams are given *after* the written examinations, the extra margin is necessary to allow for those candidates who might be disqualified by either of the two assessments. Even with these two assessments now increasingly being given prior to the written exams, however, administrators still said there were "many reasons" for retaining the extra margins, and these lie at the center of a continuing controversy. In practical terms, the margin offers the only significant space within the post-Cultural Revolution enrollment process for the manipulation by special interests, both official and otherwise, that has always characterized college admissions in China.

In this respect, the present system—at least as it existed between 1977 and 1980—was probably the least open to abuse from whatever source of any devised since 1949. But such maneuvering is still possible and continues to occur within the 15-20 percent margin. The maneuvering will, moreover, increase with the developing trend, already apparent in 1980, to grant universities greater autonomy in student admissions. One of the universities' related demands was that they be granted larger margins within which to pick and choose among the candidates. Or, in the words of one senior official: the smaller the margin, the fewer the letters of complaint from the candidates, but the greater the dissatisfaction of the universities.[15]

The Vanishing MPS

Zhejiang province deferred to the universities in this controversy by raising its margins from 15 percent to 20 percent in 1981.[16] But Shanghai and Beijing appear to be pointing the way to the future with their resolution of the controversy: authorities there simply did away with their local mps—or at least the public announcement of it. This alternative was first employed in 1980 in those two cities and apparently in some other localities as well. At least one province, Sichuan, followed suit in 1981.[17]

This change serves at once to defuse the intense interprovincial competition that has developed around the mps and to facilitate the trend toward greater university autonomy in enrollment. The costs of withdrawing the mps from public view, on the other hand, are the greater space thus allowed for internal maneuvering and public uncertainty over the standards applied. Some effort was made to address public fears about the new opportunities for "going through the back door" opened up by this development. It was explained that no mps had ever been drawn during all the years prior to the Cultural Revolution; that the mps was a post-Cultural Revolution innovation resulting largely from the need to give the physical exam after the written examinations; and that it was now no longer needed in localities which were able to give the physical prior to the examinations, as was always the sequence before 1966.[18]

In fact, it is not the mps that has been abolished but only the public announcement of it. Beijing now has a *diaodang fenshuxian*, that is, the lowest score separating the files of those who will be considered for final selection from those who will not. Tianjin uses a similar term for this line, *songdang fenshuxian*, and, unlike Beijing, was still announcing it in 1981.[19]

The physical problems of gathering and arranging the enrollment files for final selection themselves necessitate some means for separating the files of the minority, whose scores have placed them within the realm of success, from the majority who lie outside of it. Moreover, university administrators still knew the provincial rank order based on the mps in 1980, even though the official regulations had just been issued stipulating that the provinces were not to be so ranked. This, too, suggests that the mps or its equivalent is disappearing only from the public's view.

That the competition and rank ordering are continuing "internally" in some form was also suggested by the national announcement in 1981, not of the provincial mps rank order, but of the three highest-scoring candidates (identified by name, middle school, and total examination score) in each of four localities only. And these localities were the traditional high-scorers: Shanghai, Beijing, Jiangsu, and Zhejiang.[20] The reader could thus deduce that these localities once again ranked highest in 1981, as administrators admitted they had in 1980. And indeed, of the provincial mps available as shown in table 6 (p. 128), Jiangsu and Zhejiang simply exchanged places in 1981, to come in first and second, respectively.

Beijing, moreover, announced the lowest scores for the number of students roughly approximating its overall quota. In Beijing, 8,809 science candidates received scores above 390 points; 2,886 liberal arts candidates received scores above 350 points; and 612 foreign language candidates received scores above 360 points. Beijing's total enrollment quota was just over 10,000 in 1981.[21] But without more precise knowledge of just what mps was used and how large a margin they contained, candidates achieving these scores but not gaining admission to college had much weaker grounds on which to challenge their omission.

In 1982, the mps or their equivalents became even more difficult to find in the main provincial newspapers. But the *People's Daily* compiled a selection from "various papers" around the country and published them in its weekly digest.[22] This list showed Zhejiang and Jiangsu once again vying for first place:

	Sciences	Liberal Arts
Zhejiang	432 points	412 points
Jiangsu	430	410
Hunan	419	408
Liaoning	407	387
Anhui	406	397
Shandong	400	400
Guangdong	393	402
Shensi	392	389
Hebei	389	386
Nanchang	408	390
Zhengzhou	395	385
Beijing	376	383
Tianjin	360	357

In any event, the competition must continue (1) so long as the examination scores remain the main criterion governing college enrollment; and (2) especially now that the examination scores are being allowed to assume greater weight in determining admission to the key universities, as will be seen below.

The Abolition of the National MPS for Key Universities

One change indicative of the greater weight being given to the individual candidate's examination score was the elimination in 1981 of the national mps for the key universities. This mps had been drawn by the Education Ministry in roughly the same manner as the provincial mps immediately after all the examinations were graded and the provincial scores computed. The keypoint mps was determined each year at a meeting in Beijing attended by representatives from every province in early August.[23] But because it was a national score reflecting a policy decision to provide candidates from all provinces with some chance to enter the key universities and because of the variation in overall performance among the different provinces, the score had to be drawn much lower than would have resulted from the standard formula of a 15-20 percent margin beyond the total national quota of freshmen to be enrolled in all key universities. The Education Ministry deliberately tried to accommodate the interests of the low-scoring provinces with this national mps.

The key universities, as might be expected, protested the equalizing strictures of the enrollment plan and the national mps which bound them to it.[24] By 1980, changes were being introduced into this system in response to the universities' dissatisfaction with it.

The national mps for key schools marked the bottom line permissible for admission to them. These schools were not supposed to admit a candidate whose score was even a fraction of a point lower. In fact, this mps was unrealistically low for the best of the key schools and was sometimes even lower than some of the provincial mps which govern admission to ordinary institutions of higher learning. For example, the national keypoint mps in 1980 was 360 points in the sciences and 330 points in liberal arts. But first-ranked Zhejiang province's mps for ordinary schools were 374 and 365 points, respectively. Second-ranked Jiangsu had mps of 364 and 336 points, respectively. Of the universities visited, the highest *individual* mps reported in 1980 were at Fudan, with 420 points in science and 350 in liberal arts.

Because of the differing educational development of the various provinces and autonomous cities, each locality was permitted to fix its own mps for key institutions if provincial performance was such that this would be higher than the national mps. A candidate not achieving the mps set by his/her own province or city was not eligible for admission to any key school that had an assigned enrollment quota in that locality, barring a few exceptions noted below. The provincial keypoint mps contain margins of about the same size as those mentioned above for the provincial mps for ordinary schools. The provincial mps for the key schools are not generally publicized. Some of these 1980 scores revealed in the interviews are listed in table 7 (p. 129).

As with the provincial mps for ordinary colleges, each key university must theoretically enroll on the basis of these local standards, that is, the mps of each locality where the university is required by its enrollment plan to enroll students. According to this principle, the students at any single key university were being admitted on the basis of widely varying standards, at least as reflected by their entrance exam scores. In 1979, for example, the national keypoint mps was 300 points in the sciences and 310 in liberal arts, and Fujian provincial scores were the highest nationwide. Nankai University enrolled no student from that province with a score of less than 400 points but did admit a few students from Gansu whose scores were around 350 points, that being a high score in Gansu.

In 1980, however, the key schools won the right *not* to fill a portion of their fixed enrollment quotas in each province, a measure designed to improve the quality of their student bodies. The key universities were officially given the authority to drop up to 20 percent of their quotas per province, but only if that number of candidates failed to achieve *the national mps* fixed by the Education Ministry.[25]

By 1981, the trend had advanced a step further to allow the key schools to drop up to 20 percent of their provincial quotas when that number of candidates did not meet the *individual university's* admissions standards as determined by the provincial mps for key universities and each school's own minimum requirements. In fact, as will be seen below, some schools were already enrolling on this basis in 1980 in anticipation of the changing regulations and even appeared to be ignoring the provincial keypoint mps as well when this was lower than their own. With quota jumping *(tiaoming'e)* thus officially sanctioned in response to the demands of the key universities, the national unified mps ceased to perform any significant function and was abolished in 1981.[26]

Naturally, it is the borderline candidates who fall within and around this margin that are the most vulnerable as the universities pick and chose among them. And since the key schools and the many non-key schools enrolling outside their home provinces usually enroll only a handful of students in each specialty from any given province, the number of candidates "on the margin" is actually multiplied many times over. It is these borderline candidates that are most likely to be disqualified by one or more of the secondary admissions criteria as well as by the considerations of health, politics, and preference already discussed. And it is these borderline candidates that can most easily be passed over for somebody else's offspring, as the inevitable urge to beat the system seeks out this largest loophole within it.

Since the enrollment personnel must make their selections from the top down, there is usually little question about the admission of first-preference candidates who have scored in the uppermost ranges. A university which passes over such a candidate must provide the provincial enrollment committee with an explanation—required in writing by some provinces—for the decision not to admit. In such cases, the enrollment committee must give its approval to the university, without which the latter is not permitted to continue down the list of candidates to the next ten-point range.[8] Such permission is apparently not too difficult to obtain, however, since as noted the key schools can and do pass over otherwise qualified candidates with less than perfect health or political records, leaving them to the ordinary schools to accept or not as they choose.

Another consideration that can influence admissions even among higher-scoring candidates is their performance on individual subject exams, especially those related to their majors. A prospective physics major with very high scores on the physics and math exams may therefore be given preference over another candidate with a higher total score but a somewhat less impressive performance in those subjects.

The 1981 enrollment regulations also instructed the provinces to fix minimum standards for the two basic subjects of math and Chinese language; candidates failing to achieve that minimum score on either exam are automatically placed in the next lowest ten-point range. Thus if a total score is 395 points, but the math score is below standard, the candidate's file must be grouped with those in the 389-380 range rather than the 399-390 range. Some of the provincial standards fixed for these two subjects in 1981 are shown below. Zhejiang announced the standards applicable to candidates for key institutions and indicated that similar standards for other schools would be fixed appropriately. Sichuan fixed uniform standards for all schools but waived them for candidates from six specific localities with large concentrations of national minorities. Shandong also fixed uniform standards for all schools. These standards were:

	Zhejiang (key schools)[9]	*Sichuan (all schools)*[10]	*Shandong (all schools)*[11]
Science candidates			
Math	75 points	60 points	70 points
Chinese	60	60	50
Liberal arts candidates			
Math	65	50	60
Chinese	70	60	70

One administrator spoke also of a new 1980 regulation denying admission to college for any candidate with a score of less than forty points on the written politics exam. But this could not be corroborated elsewhere. Otherwise, all confirmed that it is possible to "fail" one subject exam and still gain admission to college, so long as the candidate's total score is above the mps for the locality and school in question and minimum standards for other subject examinations have been met. One candidate known to this writer was actually admitted to a liberal arts specialty in an ordinary provincial university with a score of only three points on the math exam in 1979. This question is complicated, however, by the definition of what constitutes a failing score. According to Chinese pedagogical custom, sixty points or less is regarded as failing, but this standard is not necessarily applied to the college entrance examinations. One province, for example, specified that forty points would be regarded as a passing grade on a certain subject exam.[12] Clearly, the definition is flexible and open to change as the need arises.

Starting in 1980, new regulations decreed that preference within the ten-point range is supposed to be given to candidates who have been named "three-good" students (that is, good in studies, health, and politics/deportment) in middle school for two consecutive years and to student cadres. Administrators insisted that despite the overwhelming preponderance of Communist Youth League members among the successful candidates at all the universities visited, ordinary CYL members were not given preference in admission unless they had also achieved three-good status or served as student cadres in middle school.

Administrators in both the universities and middle schools professed to find no political significance in the large proportions of CYL members among the graduating seniors of key middle schools and the freshmen at key universities. As one university administrator explained, the CYL is still a political organization, only its political goals have changed. "Now the political goal is to work for the four modernizations and the most important thing a student can do is to study well." Hence, if students do not have good grades, they cannot become members of the CYL. Similarly, young factory workers cannot be admitted for membership unless they are "good producers," doing their jobs without errors or defects. It therefore follows that students whose grades are high enough to gain admission to a key university would also have been admitted to the CYL on the same grounds.[13]

Thus negligible political significance appears to have been attached to CYL membership by 1980. This would explain the turn to other criteria such as those represented by the three-good students. By inserting them into the enrollment regulations, the Ministry of Education was acknowledging the criticism that had developed—both in China itself and from foreign sources—over the overwhelming reliance on the entrance examination scores alone as the chief criterion for admission to college.

Administrators could provide little evidence of any special advantage actually accruing to student cadres and three-good students in the admission process, except to mention that preference was supposed to be given them. Nevertheless, official pressure to give such preference has continued. Sichuan province, for example, actually proclaimed a new regulation in 1981, *raising* the score by one ten-point range for all candidates who had placed in the competitions evaluating each school's three-good students on all-city and all-prefectural levels. Also to be so rewarded were candidates who excel in similar competitions each year to honor the best CYL members, student cadres, and sports contestants. This made it possible for a young woman who was an all-city three-good student in Chongqing to gain admission to the Chinese Science and Technology University with an entrance exam score of 469 points, when that school could have filled its Sichuan quota with first-preference candidates scoring no lower than 470 points.[14]

Because of the new national regulation, however, "not a few" middle schools in one province—Shandong—were reported to be relaxing the requirements for naming three-good students. The schools were doing so in order to guarantee as many of their students as possible the extra advantage such status could bring and thus push up pass rates. Schools were also "relaxing the conditions for admission to the CYL" and simply giving membership to students on the basis of their grades alone.[15] The phrasing of this report implies a somewhat different interpretation of CYL admissions requirements than that conveyed by the university administrator cited above.

Administrators reported variously on the weight given to middle school grades alone; some said they were used for reference only and "played no deciding role," while others claimed they might influence the decision to admit in marginal cases. One such example was a science candidate at Nanjing University in 1980, the first year that Jiangsu province began to consider middle school grades. This candidate's total entrance exam score was acceptable, but he had scored only eighty-nine points on the math exam, a borderline grade by the standards Nan-da likes to maintain on that individual exam for science candidates. It was his consistently high grades in his middle school mathematics courses that finally swung the decision in this candidate's favor.[16]

Additional unpublicized factors also influence the decision to enroll one candidate over another. One of these is officially sanctioned although not included in the official enrollment regulations. This is the linked middle school preference scheme mentioned in Chapter III. The related university will give candidates from its associated middle school preference *(youxuan)* over others of equal qualification, equal meaning *within the ten-point range*. Thus if there is only one remaining place to be filled in French at Fudan, and one of the candidates in the final ten-point range to be considered is from one of Fudan's linked middle schools, while other candidates in the same range are not, the former will be enrolled.[17]

Other "criteria" that move into operation at this time are not officially sanctioned but appear to be condoned in practice. For example, one university vice-president insisted that, other qualifications being equal within the same ten-point range, the children of the university's own faculty and staff are given preference over all others, including workers' children. Indeed, it was the university's socialist responsibility to look after its own in this manner. Administrators elsewhere denied that this was the practice in their schools but did volunteer that this kind of preference in selection was one of the few areas within the present enrollment system where it was still possible to exert "back-door" influence.

These administrators further acknowledged that this sort of influence is most easily exercised by university people themselves since it requires direct access to any given school's enrollment personnel. Thus a member of a university's enrollment team may be approached to "look after" *(zhaogu)* someone's son or daughter. This can be done most easily within the ten-point score range, but increasingly beyond it as well, aided by the 15-20 percent "pass" margins, quota jumping, and related practices.

For example, there could be a number of considerations that an enrollment worker might choose to challenge for any candidate whose political record was not absolutely "clear"; or who had not received an unconditionally clean bill of health on the physical exam; or who had scored a few points below standard on a major subject exam. The enrollment worker has the power to overlook such considerations or to use them as a pretext for disqualifying one candidate to create an opening for another. This practice of deliberately creating an opening for some relevant person's offspring is widely acknowledged by administrators and teachers familiar with the enrollment system. They also generally condone it on the grounds that to benefit from this kind of "consideration," the other candidate must at least have achieved a competitive score on the entrance examinations.

A good example of this kind of "back-door" manipulation by cadres and university officials was provided by a Hong Kong friend after a visit home to China at enrollment time in August 1982. It involved the case of an acquaintance who is a leading cadre in a municipal education bureau and whose son had just scored several points below the mps of his first-preference college, located in the same city. As it happened, the father was a long-time friend and colleague of the college president, who personally agreed to see to it that the son was enrolled. This also vindicated the parents' game-plan; they had dissuaded the son from writing as his first preference a school in a distant city where they knew no one and so had no network of connections to rely on should the need arise.

Clearly, the system has room for such manipulations, and it is being further enhanced through: (1) the universities' successful demands for larger rather than smaller "pass" margins, which create larger pools of candidates from which to choose; (2) the vanishing mps; (3) the consequent growing secrecy in the standards applied; and (4) the increasing autonomy in selection being granted to the individual universities themselves.

Quota Jumping (tiaoming'e)

Perhaps the most significant development along these lines is the already mentioned practice of quota jumping, officially sanctioned in 1980. None of the universities could provide statistics on the number of candidates affected by the new regulation. Shandong University claimed not even to have tried to avail itself of the new privilege, which has apparently not received an overly enthusiastic welcome from the provinces. In 1980, at least, the province to be slighted had to agree to waive its quota, and if the province refused, the university was required to appeal the provincial decision and obtain permission from the Education Ministry.[18]

With the practice only just announced and controversial, the universities were understandably reluctant to discuss it. Moreover, some of the related practices they were even then developing to "force up quality" were still bordering on the fringes of illegality. The public announcement authorizing these practices was not made until 1981 in conjunction with the revised regulations on quota jumping for keypoint institutions and the abolition of their national mps. These practices are outlined in brief below.

The universities are now allowed to drop as much as 20 percent of their quotas in any given province if the university itself decides this is necessary to guarantee quality *(baozheng zhiliang)*. Thus freed from the full constraints of their quotas, the key universities are now a step closer to setting their own admissions standards. They view the links with elite middle schools as a means toward this end, as is the method of *estimating* their own individual university's mps each year. This latter procedure provides a way to determine exactly what is necessary to "guarantee quality."

Individual schools do not fix their mps; the lowest permissible score is not known until the last student is enrolled. Nevertheless, the key universities were in 1980 using advance information from their local enrollment committees to help determine their annual admissions standards. This advance information is based on the patterns of enrollment apparent since 1977. As noted, the most popular universities for the majority of candidates are those closest to home. Hence, most of the best students—except for the very brightest who can aspire to attend Beijing or Qinghua universities—will be applying to a few universities within their own home provinces (or autonomous cities). On the basis of this pattern, some universities had already developed, in effect, a dual set of standards: one for local students and one for those from outside provinces, with the latter usually lower than the former. Given below, for example, are the *actual* —not anticipated—1980 mps for one university visited, with the contrasting 1980 national mps for key schools and the local mps for non-key schools in the university's home province:

	Sciences	*Liberal Arts*
Mps of home-province candidates	400 points	360 points
Mps of out-of-province candidates	377	346
Mps of national key schools	360	330
Mps of provincial non-key schools (approx.)	350	330

With this pattern generally although not universally well developed, the provincial enrollment office will, before selection work begins, provide the key schools with an informal estimate of what its mps will be for local candidates. This estimate is made on the basis of the scores of those local candidates who have chosen the university as their first preference. A university can then use that *estimated* mps as a guideline against which to evaluate candidates from outside provinces. If communications are well developed, outside provinces may also provide such advance information to the university. In this manner, Zhongshan University learned in 1980, for instance, that its home-province scores were *not* actually going to be higher than out-of-province scores that year. It is against these advance guidelines that a key university will be able to make decisions concerning the number of candidates that are beneath its admissions standards and should therefore be passed over in order to "guarantee quality."

Theoretically, such information should have been of little use before 1981 because, according to the national regulations, the key universities could only drop a portion of their quotas when the candidates fell beneath the *national* mps fixed by the Ministry of Education. But the key universities were at least using the information (whether advance or *ex post facto*) on the number of high-scoring local students who had to be rejected in order to enroll lower-scoring outside students, to substantiate their demands for some release from the quota system. The demands have now been at least partially met with the "legalization" of the use to which some key universities were already putting their advance information in 1980.

Of the localities visited, Shanghai's universities appeared to be the most advanced in terms of the development and use of this "early-warning system." Administrators spelled out the circumstances that have made this possible for Fudan University: (1) Shanghai scores can be computed faster than those of a province; (2) the best of Fudan's students always originate in Shanghai; (3) the majority of its yearly enrollment quota is from Shanghai itself; and (4) a majority of the best students in the city apply to enter Fudan.

With this knowledge, Fudan was able to use its *estimated* mps, drawn on the basis of the scores of its first-preference Shanghai candidates, to select students from outlying areas. These "must meet the Shanghai standard," or Fudan will not admit them. For example, Fudan decided in 1980, on the basis of the Shanghai scores, that it could fill the university's physics quota without dropping below a total score on the entrance examination of 440 points. Fudan's enrollment representatives were therefore sent out with instructions to admit no student to the physics department with anything lower. (Fudan's final all-school mps that year was 420 points for science and 350 points for liberal arts; the "average score" in the sciences was around 440.)

Using its own high standards—and not the lower national mps or even the Shanghai key schools' mps—Fudan was in 1980 already engaged in quota jumping, enrolling "a bit more or less" of its assigned quotas in different localities. If the first-preference candidates in an outlying province did "not adversely affect the standards" fixed on the basis of the Shanghai first-preference scores, Fudan would enroll its full quota in the outlying province; otherwise, Fudan would make up the difference elsewhere.[19]

Wuhan University similarly claimed to be setting its own individual standards prior to selection (400 points for the sciences in 1980) and further indicated that it did not have to accept candidates with lower scores in order to fill its provincial quotas.[20] East China Teachers' Training University also claimed to have indulged in quota jumping, although it was still enrolling "basically according to the plan."[21]

None of these three schools mentioned adhering to a limit of 20 percent on quota adjustments (as required by the official regulations), nor was there any reference to using the lower national mps as the guideline. Administrators elsewhere subsequently pronounced such methods "illegal," and the Shanghai press stated clearly that "schools must not fix their own standards."[22] The practice was nevertheless authorized by the revised regulations on quota adjustments issued in 1981.

The one remaining obstacle to the implementation of these regulations is provincial resistance. In the words of one administrator, the provinces "do not like to give their permission" for quota jumping. The interests of the province lie always in the enrollment of as many native sons and daughters as possible in the best schools. For this reason, according to one report from Jiangsu following enrollment in 1981, quota revisions were not substantial. That province, one of the highest scoring in the country, was able to add only eleven places in key universities as a result of quotas dropped elsewhere.[23]

Sichuan, with a lower reputed performance rating, lost some forty places in key institutions outside the province but picked up a few seats in others. Meanwhile, first-category schools within the province actually exceeded their quotas by a total of ninety, in accordance with the regulation allowing universities to exceed their enrollment quotas by from 1 to 3 percent. The result was a net gain for Sichuan of fifty-six students over its planned 1981 quota for first-category institutions.[24]

Enrollment Planning and the Educationally Underprivileged

As might be expected given the trends described above, the key universities are required to make few concessions "of quality" for the disadvantaged sectors of Chinese society. Prior to the Cultural Revolution, administrators recalled, enrollment policies varied, sometimes requiring quotas or ratios for students of worker-peasant origin but at other times requiring only that they be given preference over other candidates of equal qualification. All such measures are currently regarded as remnants of the radical Maoist past and have not been restored. There were in 1980 no mandatory or fixed ratios for such students in any kind of school. One administrator did acknowledge this as "a problem" particularly with respect to rural students since few were now being admitted to college. But he explained that official policy now aimed only at gradually improving the level of education in the countryside; as part of that effort rural schools were actually being closed and enrollments curtailed in accordance with the reorganization of secondary education. The net result, at least for the time being therefore, was to "write off" the rural areas as a source of college students.

Administrators pointed out that any responsibilities the key schools had in terms of educating the disadvantaged were fulfilled primarily through the national enrollment plan itself. Until 1980 the key universities were assigned, in accordance with this plan, fixed numbers of students from low-scoring provinces where, as one administrator noted, their enrollment representatives would never have ventured if left to themselves. A quota of ten students for

Zhongshan University from Ningxia province was a case in point. As already indicated, the varying provincial mps have been used as indicators of the varying levels of "educational development," with scores generally lower in the hinterland and higher in the coastal provinces. Thus were it not for the balance built into the national plan, even more students would be enrolled in the key schools from the high-scoring coastal provinces than has otherwise been the case.

But as we have also seen, the key universities dislike the imposition these lower-scoring students represent and lobbied for larger quotas from the higher-scoring provinces, as well as the right to jump the quotas themselves when the number of high-scoring candidates is not sufficient to fill them. Hence the 1980 decision to begin releasing these universities from some of the confines of their fixed quotas in the lower-scoring provinces is yet another step away from the spirit of the more egalitarian enrollment policies of the past. But in this case it occurs at the expense of the educationally underdeveloped regions and provinces as a whole—rather than any particular social group—which stand to lose what the elite schools gain.

Administrators asserted that, in fact, within the total provincial quotas the major responsibility for accommodating the disadvantaged areas lies directly with the ordinary provincial institutions of higher learning and, among them, primarily with the junior colleges. Yet here again, that responsibility is discharged mainly through the balance built into the predetermined enrollment plans.

As noted at the outset of this report, the precise formula for fixing the national enrollment plan was not revealed. But the provincial quotas which make up its sum total represent an attempt to balance the supply of college seats, the needs of the various provinces, and the educational development of each. Thus, the total provincial quota of educationally developed Zhejiang only in part reflects its high performance rating; while Gansu's quota within the overall national plan will not be directly proportional to its generally lower examination scores.

The center hands down to the provinces the aggregate quotas for freshman enrollment in provincial institutions each year. The provincial education bureaus are responsible for dividing up these quotas and assigning them to the various schools under their jurisdiction, in the same manner that the Education Ministry fixes the enrollment quotas for each key university. The enrollment quotas are thus seen as the chief means of granting "preference" in college admissions, both to educationally backward provinces and to such districts within provinces. But precisely how such quotas are assigned both between provinces and within them; what formulas are used for drawing the local mps; what principles are applied in enrollment work; and how rigorously these are enforced—all of these questions fall within the preserve of national and provincial education authorities, who unfortunately could not be interviewed for this study.

The evidence suggests, however, that it is not just the key schools that have sought to raise their entrance requirements. The pressures to push up the provincial mps have also been intense and have extended throughout the system. This has resulted in some junior college mps that are not significantly lower than those, for regular colleges. The efforts to curb this competitive drive have been mentioned, as have the continuing pressures to the contrary, which work against unified attempts to accommodate educationally backward sectors and districts.

In any case, the administrators interviewed said only that they themselves had no direct experience with the enrollment of such candidates, since it was not a matter that concerned their universities. They claimed to have only hearsay knowledge of this task and according to that knowledge, it is primarily into the most basic-level junior colleges that the lowest-scoring candidates—whatever their origins—are now being channeled.

In sum, the key universities were subject to no fixed quotas or ratios for any category of student. Nor were worker-peasant students, favored in the past, granted any form of preference on grounds of class origin in any kind of college or university. The problem of the educationally disadvantaged is now seen essentially as one of regional imbalance in the development of education and not, as previously, of social inequalities between town and countryside or between intellectuals and the working class. Consistent with this diagnosis, the problem is currently being addressed primarily through the provincial balance built into the annual unified enrollment plan and the hierarchy of institutions it serves. The 1983 national enrollment regulations further acknowledged this division of labor. They stipulated, for example, that junior colleges specializing in agriculture, forestry, medicine, and teacher training should enroll primarily within their own prefectures, should draw their minimum passing scores on that basis, and should train their students for job assignments within the locality.

Enrollment Preferences for the More and Less Advantaged

Nevertheless, there are a variety of preferential principles and practices—only a few of which have yet been mentioned—which are supposed to be followed by enrollment personnel during final selection. Four different methods may be used in granting different degrees of preference to different kinds of students as their examination scores appear in the final line-up for selection by any given school. These methods are: (1) the already mentioned preferred enrollment *(youxuan luqu)* when all other conditions are comparable, usually within the ten-point range; (2) lowering or expanding *(fangkuang)* the passing score, that is, allowing a flexible or floating passing score in some cases; (3)

establishing a fixed lower score for certain kinds of candidates *(jiangdi fenshu)*; and (4) making special exceptions or "selecting the best from among the lowest" (sometimes referred to as *zeyou zhaogu)*.

The kinds of candidates for whom preferred enrollment within the ten-point range is officially sanctioned are: (1) students from the associated or linked middle schools; (2) students awarded the three-good title for two consecutive years in middle school; (3) students who have served as cadres in middle school; (4) students who have achieved the national physical fitness standards; (5) candidates from Overseas Chinese families or from Taiwan; and (6) members of China's national minorities living outside minority autonomous areas. Students meeting any one of these criteria are supposed to be given preference in admission over others of comparable qualifications within the ten-point range. All of these preferences are officially sanctioned in the national enrollment regulations, with the exception of that authorized under the linked middle-schools preference scheme, which has not yet been publicly announced.

Another rule, this one concerning women candidates, also has not yet been publicized. Women are included within this same category of preference, but in a certain obverse manner: if a female candidate's qualifications are equal to others within a ten-point range, a school is not supposed to deny admission to her simply because of her sex. This cautionary rule is designed to counteract the widely reported local custom of raising the passing grade for girls and women in secondary school and college admissions and on employment qualification examinations. Tianjin, for example, fixed an mps of 220 points for boys but 230 for girls on the entrance examination for its secondary vocational schools in 1980.[25]

This form of preferred enrollment, all other conditions being equal within a ten-point range, is essentially a device for selecting from among the equally advantaged and is a general principle which all schools, both keypoint and ordinary, are supposed to follow where applicable. None of the universities could, however, provide any indication as to how extensive their application of this principle was or the kinds and numbers of students affected by it.

The three other means of granting preference can be applied to a variety of candidates. But one of the main objectives in actually lowering standards—rather than merely giving preference among equals—is to encourage candidates to enter unpopular fields of study. The aim of benefiting the disadvantaged is served as a corollary, however, since it is the lower-scoring students who are thereby channeled into the less popular fields. In 1980 and 1981, schools enrolling in geology, petroleum technology, agronomy, forestry, and teacher training could apply flexible standards *(fangkuang)* as necessary to fill their enrollment quotas. By 1983, military academies and maritime transport had been added to the list and first-preference candidates were offered preferred enrollment *(zeyou luqu)*.

In deference to the problem of recruiting into unpopular fields of study, the enrollment regulations from 1978 through 1980 had also stipulated that preference within the ten-point range could be given by institutions specializing in mining and petroleum technology, geology, forestry, and agriculture to employees already working in those fields and to the graduates of middle schools run by related enterprises. Such middle schools serve only the children of the enterprise's employees. Agriculture and forestry colleges were also authorized to give such preference to educated rural youth and to city youth sent down to the countryside; while medical colleges could give preference in enrollment to barefoot doctors, and teacher training schools to rural teachers. By 1983, these particular preferences had been rephrased into a simpler acknowledgment that the only means of filling enrollment quotas in certain fields was, in effect, by heredity. Mining, geology, and petroleum schools were instructed to lower *(jiangdi)* their admissions scores and enroll "appropriately" from within these respective systems, and return students to them upon graduation. A similar ruling for rural students in rural specialties was noted above.[26]

The principle of lowering the passing score is also applied uniformly when admitting candidates from the national minority districts and regions. As indicated, where national minorities live scattered among the Han Chinese population, minority candidates are only supposed to be given preference when their performance is otherwise comparable to Han candidates.

There has also been a provision that in any single county where no candidates achieve the mps, an exception can be made and "some" students can nevertheless be enrolled *(zeyou zhaogu)*. The objective is that no county, no matter how low its candidates' scores, should fail to have some representatives entering college each year. The provinces fix their own specific rules in accordance with the more general national regulations issued annually. On this latter point, for example, Sichuan province stipulated in 1981 that in any county where less than three new students had been enrolled, places "could" be found for up to three of that county's highest-scoring candidates.[27]

Administrators at the universities visited were generally reticent to clarify the extent to which their own schools applied any of the latter three preferential enrollment practices. The motivation for their reticence was never entirely clear. At the East China Teachers' Training University, it might have been related to an unwillingness to reveal how much the standards had had to be lowered in order to fill the annual enrollment quotas due to the unpopularity of teacher training schools. Elsewhere, the silence on this subject sometimes seemed to be due to a similar unwillingness to admit that the standards of a keypoint university had actually been compromised in this manner; while at other times it appeared related to the administrators' embarrassment at the infrequency with which the principles were applied—particularly when it was assumed that the foreign investigator thought they should be.

With respect to the special exceptions made for some low-scoring candidates, the administrators all asserted convincingly that they had no knowledge of such enrollments because these were the responsibility of the non-key provincial schools and especially of the junior colleges. Hence, no one knew how the regulation concerning educationally backward counties was implemented. It was explained that when no candidate in a county achieves the provincial mps, responsibility for handling the problem lies with the enrollment office of the province, which usually assigns such county candidates to junior-college courses. Theoretically, it would be possible for a provincial enrollment office to ask a key university—or even an ordinary provincial school, such as Jiangxi Gong-da was in the process of becoming—to make an exception and accept a few such low-scoring county candidates after regular enrollment had been completed. But no school visited including the latter would admit to receiving or even being asked to receive any such students.

The administrators claimed further that there were neither fixed ratios nor mandatory rules governing the application of these principles that would require the key universities to lower their standards for any category of student. The Ministry of Education was said by the university administrators to have stipulated that each key school could do as it liked in this matter. The ministry spokesman, on the other hand, said that in 1978 some of the key schools had made special exceptions for national minority candidates, admitting some with scores well below that year's national keypoint mps. But by 1980, he said, the power of the key universities was "so great" that when the ministry again asked them to make such special exceptions, they refused, and "the ministry had no way to make them do it."

Thus the key schools would admit to relaxing *their own individual* admissions standards only in rare circumstances. Even though the lower national mps for key schools was still being drawn in 1980, these schools were apparently not using it as the standard against which to admit low-scoring students. The measures acknowledged were primarily applications of the preference principle within the ten-point range, as the following reports show.

Shandong University reported giving preference within the ten-point range only to candidates with Overseas Chinese connections, including those from Taiwan, Hong Kong, and Macao, and to national minority candidates. But the numbers actually enrolled in this manner were not revealed.[28]

Administrators at Zhongshan University explained that the files of all the above were kept separately for consideration during the final selection process. But the university would not even consider enrolling anyone beneath the national mps for key schools. While it might relax admissions standards by ten to twenty points for such students, this move would be based on the university's own individual standards, not the lower national mps. In 1977, for example, Zhongshan made such an exception for one national minority candidate in the sciences whose score was above the mps but lower than that of any other student enrolled in that particular specialty that year. And, in fact, the university had only a "few" minority students. Zhongshan administrators also pointed out that since lower-scoring Overseas Chinese students once again had their own schools—Jinan University in Guangzhou and the Overseas Chinese University in Fujian—there was no need to make special exceptions for them at a key school such as Zhongshan. Hence that university had "only one or two" students from Hong Kong and Macao.[29]

The 1981 Guangdong provincial enrollment regulations seemed to corroborate this report. They specified only that provincial colleges had the responsibility of lowering their mps by twenty points for minority candidates and by ten points for Han candidates who had attended two years or more of senior middle school in a minority district.[30]

Nanjing University also indicated that it would admit minorities and Overseas Chinese only if they met Nan-da's own standards. As a consequence, only one student from Macao was admitted in 1979, and none was enrolled in 1980. Lower-scoring students, regardless of their origins, would not in any case apply to Nan-da since they would know they had no chance of being admitted there.[31] East China Teachers' Training University in 1980 enrolled eight students in physical education with "lower" entrance exam scores but would not reveal how much lower, nor acknowledge any other exceptions.[32]

Fudan University claimed to treat all minorities and Overseas Chinese candidates in the same manner as those from its linked middle schools: all other qualifications being equal, they would be granted preference within a ten-point range. But Fudan is unwilling to lower its standards for anyone because "if we let in a few, then everyone would want to come here." As of 1980, Fudan had a total of five thousand undergraduates, of whom only "about twenty" were national minorities and an additional three were Overseas Chinese from Hong Kong.[33]

The very small number of candidates who are actually affected by the principle of giving preference within a ten-point range is exemplified by the 1980 enrollment statistics for the entire city of Shanghai. Only fifty-two candidates of national minority, Taiwanese and Overseas Chinese origin were enrolled on this basis among the more than ten thousand students admitted to Shanghai's forty-four institutions of higher learning that year.[34]

Only two universities would actually admit to lowering their standards. Wuhan University, citing "problems created each year by Yunnan, Guizhou, and Guangxi" (traditionally among the lower-scoring provinces and having relatively large concentrations of national minorities), claimed to reduce its own mps by ten points for candidates from these three provinces. Similarly, candidates from other provinces who were members of China's national minorities could be granted this same ten-point bonus, but only if they were from a national minority district. The rule, moreover, was that no more than 1 percent of Wuhan University's students could be enrolled in this manner.[35]

Lanzhou University claimed that it made special exceptions only for candidates with Overseas Chinese connections, including those from Hong Kong, Macao, and Taiwan. In 1978, when the national mps for the key universities was 340 points, this university enrolled two Overseas Chinese candidates from Fujian province with scores of 302 points and 289 points.

Lanzhou University also claimed to lower its mps for national minority candidates by ten or twenty points but could provide no specific information on its own specific practices in this regard. Presumably, they are not extensive, since this university, which serves primarily a region with a sizable minority population, provided enrollment statistics to show that its yearly intake of minority students actually declined from 32 students in 1976 (total freshman enrollment was 845) to 14 students in 1979 (out of 1,060 freshmen enrolled).[36]

In fact, the lower-scoring national minority candidates can now be admitted to any one of the ten different national minorities institutes around the country. These are located, for the most part, in areas of minority concentrations.[37] These institutes are run on the assumption that the national minorities—of which there are now officially fifty-five distinct groups with a total population of approximately 60 million[38]—are generally less educationally advanced than the dominant Han majority. Hence, both the curriculum and admissions standards of the minorities institutes reflect that assumption. The special "separate and less equal" status of these schools was yet another target of the Cultural Revolution, and they remained closed much longer than most other institutions of higher learning. By the mid-1970s, some of the minorities institutes were functioning again. Now, of course, they are fully rehabilitated.

The Northwest National Minorities Institute in Lanzhou had enrolled students with scores of 190 points on the college entrance examinations in 1979. That year, the national mps for key schools was 310 points in liberal arts and 300 for the sciences, while the provincial Gansu mps for non-key schools was 270 points.[39]

The key universities are now encouraged to run special separate classes for minorities, the admissions scores of which can also be lowered "appropriately." None of the universities visited was running such a class in 1980, but Zhongshan University did apparently establish one the following year.[40]

One province, Sichuan, published fairly detailed enrollment regulations in 1981, and these shed greater light on the implementation of the various enrollment principles, at least with respect to national minorities. The Sichuan regulations applied specifically to candidates from the three towns, two counties, and one district in the province that have large concentrations of minorities. First-category universities were permitted to lower their standards by twenty points for national minority candidates from these six localities and by ten points for Han Chinese from the same areas. Second-category schools could lower their standards by forty points and twenty points, respectively. Minority candidates living in predominantly Han localities were to be given preference only within the ten-point range. Unfortunately, the published regulations did not indicate: whether these were mandatory or only suggested guidelines; the number of students that any given school was expected to enroll in this manner; or which standard—the provincial or that of each individual school—the minority candidates' scores were to be measured against.

In addition, at least 80 percent of the Sichuan quota at the Southwest National Minorities Institute in Chengdu had to be filled by minority candidates; only Han Chinese from the six specified localities could fill the remainder of Sichuan's total quota at that institute. Three junior colleges—two specializing in education and one in agriculture—were "in principle" to concentrate enrollment in the six localities, and at least 25 percent of their new students had to be of national minority origin. Finally, Sichuan also temporarily waived the new 1981 minimum requirements for the Chinese language and math exams for candidates from the six localities.[41]

Admissions Scores

As has been noted, the universities were not willing to contribute specific data to show precisely how they might be implementing these general enrollment principles. Similarly, most of the universities visited were reluctant to reveal their actual mps or provide data on the range of their freshman entrance examination scores. This information is treated as something of an "organization secret," which circulates internally and which candidates do their best to discover and pass on from year to year but which is rarely publicized. The key universities, at least, guard this secret with some care, since their reputations now lie in maintaining as high a minimum passing score as possible on the one hand, while on the other they claim to need that necessary "margin for maneuver" at the borderline.

Only two universities, Jilin and Jiangxi Gong-da, were willing to provide any statistics on admissions scores. Unfortunately, neither school's data are sufficient to illustrate the extent to which they may be relaxing requirements for different kinds of students. The range of scores provided by Jilin University shows only that it was willing to make one exception for a student beneath the national keypont mps and that it did enroll a number of "marginal" students in the 310-320 point range, which a school like Fudan University apparently would not. The Jiangxi Gong-da figures show that its students have a comparatively low performance rating on the entrance exams, as might be expected since Jiangxi Gong-da enrolls as a second-category or ordinary school on an intra-provincial basis only. Nevertheless, 58 percent of its 1980 freshmen scored above the national keypoint mps, while all of the remainder apparently scored no more than 5 points below it. The admissions scores for these two universities are shown in table 9 (p. 130).

Expanded Enrollment

There is one category of lower-scoring student which the key universities are, however, enrolling. These are primarily local urban students admitted to courses at the junior-college level *(zhuanke).* These are part of the various expanded enrollment programs which even the key schools are now required to run. Such programs have been devised as virtually the only means of cutting through the fixed patterns of university life to tap some of the underutilized manpower and facilities therein. The commuter student must be the target of this effort since the universities could not undertake it otherwise without substantial increased investment in new campus housing and the already overburdened logistical support system.[42]

In 1977 and 1978, relatively large numbers of students were admitted to college in this manner after the predetermined enrollment plan had been filled. These figures are shown in table 10 (p. 131). By the 1980-81 academic year, such extra-quota students constituted approximately 10 percent of all college enrollment, or 112,800 students out of a total of 1,143,700. The two cities of Shanghai and Beijing accounted for almost 30 percent of the total expanded enrollment.

The enrollment of extra-quota students was announced with some fanfare in early 1978 when a circular from the Education Ministry and the State Planning Commission was issued urging regular institutions of higher learning to admit more students wherever possible.[43] The 1978 commuter students were enrolled under a variety of programs. The most problematic appears to have been one which permitted such students to attend daytime courses together with regular students.

One administrator at the Beijing Teachers' Training University advised dourly that there was no need even to ask about this program; it had only been experimental and was generally regarded to have failed, since all the 1978 commuter students had already moved on campus. Administrators at several other universities spoke of the problems these students had caused with their complaints about the inconveniences of daily commuting into the suburbs, where most universities are located. And these universities, too, reported that most or all of their 1978 commuters had been allowed to move on campus as dormitory space became available for them.

Few commuter students were admitted in 1979, and when such enrollments were resumed in 1980, they were governed by more stringent rules to prevent the sort of integration achieved by the earlier group. Under the new rules, only students actually living within easy commuting distance of the university were to be enrolled as commuters. But as a result, some administrators pointed out, it was the university's own faculty and staff children who stood to benefit most from the commuter program. This was particularly true for campuses located in more isolated suburban locations. Indeed, in 1980, Fudan University set up a commuter night-school on campus expressly for the children of university personnel who had otherwise failed to gain admission. It enrolled 249 tuition-paying students whose entrance examination scores were "a bit lower" than those of regular Fudan undergraduates.[44]

All together, twenty-four institutions of higher learning in Shanghai enrolled commuter students in 1980. The majority of the three thousand students admitted on this basis were enrolled in two- or three-year specialized junior-college courses. It was announced in advance that these students would be responsible for expenses usually borne primarily by the state, such as food, transportation, medical care, books and supplies, and tuition. Moreover, the graduates of these programs will not be eligible for job placement under the national unified plan nor will the city guarantee their employment. The school will be responsible for "introducing" those who can qualify for graduation to work units which can select them or not according to their needs and the students' qualifications.[45] The tuition figures most frequently mentioned for such students were in the range of 20-30 *rmb* per person per semester. The highest tuition reported was for commuter students in Changchun, who paid 10 *rmb* per month.[46]

Several other provinces announced the resumption of expanded enrollments through similar kinds of commuter programs, including Zhejiang, Anhui, Shaanxi, Guangdong, and Henan.[47] If the total figures announced for such enrollments (shown in table 10) are accurate, however, 1980 admissions on this basis were not extensive.

Another innovation, the branch college, offers a solution to one of the commuter students' problems. Universities and colleges located in the suburbs of Wuhan, for example, are setting up branch campuses in town (six, with a total of 1,600 students, by late 1980). By contrast, Nanjing University, located in the city center, was trying to decide whether to establish a branch campus in a distant suburban county.

Much publicity also attended the 1978 inauguration of the branch campus experiment. It began—in its post-Cultural Revolution form—in Tianjin and is said to have been the inspiration of then Tianjin Party Secretary Lin Hujia. Several of the universities visited had established such branches or were in the process of doing so by late 1980. They now appear to be most numerous in Beijing, perhaps reflecting Lin's subsequent tenure as mayor of that city. By mid-1980, Beijing had thirty-six branch campuses with a total enrollment of 17,440 students.[48] Considerable effort has been expended to promote these schools and to dispel some of the aura of inferiority that clearly hangs over them.[49] One consequent variation is the "commuter university," at least three of which have been set up in the cities of Chengdu, Changchun, and Hefei.[50]

Local financial resources are used to set up and maintain these branch campuses. They enroll only local commuter students under conditions similar to those described above for expanded-enrollment commuter students at the main campus. But the branches appear to maintain varying degrees of contact with and reliance on the parent school. Administrators at Fudan University claimed the relationship with its branch exists in name only and anticipated that even that link would soon be severed. The branch was set up in great haste by the city in 1979, which turned to Fudan for the use of its name and a few of its teachers. Otherwise, leadership, personnel, development, teaching, curriculum, finance, student enrollment, and job assignment were all managed independently by the city administration. Administrators at Beijing Teachers' Training University described its two branches in only slightly less detached terms and therefore claimed to have little knowledge of their operations.

By contrast, Nankai University's branch maintained a much closer relationship with the main campus and was located in a building just adjacent to it. Some 110 of the total 150 teachers at the branch were from the main campus, drawn mainly from among the younger teachers. The parent university was responsible for personnel, curriculum development, and teaching. Finance, construction, planning, and development were the responsibility of the city Communist Party committee, which in Tianjin were still directly responsible for university administration in 1980. Students from the branch school were permitted to use main campus facilities, including the library, laboratories, playing fields, and dining halls.

While the branches were all intended for extra-quota students initially, some localities appear now to be incorporating the branches into their enrollment plans, and so it is difficult to determine what the future status of these schools is to be. Administrators at the Nankai University Branch School said the long-term plan was to build the school into a new independent college run by the city. But whatever their status within the enrollment plan, all branch campus students are local commuters; they do not qualify for employment under the national unified job-assignment plan; and they are enrolled with lower minimum passing scores than are used for regular students at the parent campus. Some of these separate mps for the commuter and branch campus students are shown in table 11 (p. 132).

CHAPTER VI

Who Benefits?

Few statistical profiles of the freshman classes have been issued to confirm or deny the impressionistic accounts now circulating in China about whose children are gaining admission to college. Since all of the relevant information is contained in full in the files of every candidate and college student, the apparent reluctance to compile and/or publicize it most likely reflects the controversy that surrounds the question of access to a college education, one of the most valued objectives in Chinese society. This single question has been the focal point of all the changing enrollment policies over the years.

Reference has already been made to the direction of these policies.[1] To summarize here, during the Cultural Revolution decade and for many years prior to it as well, the aim was to enroll increasing numbers of working-class students to ensure that they too shared access to the privilege of a college education. The methods for doing this varied, but university administrators recalled that prior to 1966, their enrollment quotas were sometimes fixed to ensure the admission of a certain proportion of students from working-class families.

Enrollment policies were also implemented increasingly as the Cultural Revolution approached to discriminate against students with "bad" family backgrounds whether so designated for reasons of class or simply of politics. By 1966, the main categories of young people who were either being deprived of the right to attend college or whose access was in some way restricted were those whose circle of immediate relatives contained: capitalists, landlords, rich peasants, convicted criminals, counterrevolutionaries both historical and current, rightist intellectuals, and those who had committed other kinds of serious political errors variously defined at different times.

During the Cultural Revolution decade, these rules continued to be applied to the detriment of such young people. Opinions vary on the expansion of the categories during that time. Some say the discrimination was extended to the families of all intellectuals and the relations of Overseas Chinese. Others say these two groups were not discriminated against *per se*. It only seemed that way because most individuals within them were either rightists or of bad class background.

In any event, the beneficiaries during the Cultural Revolution decade continued to be the children of workers, peasants, and cadres with "clear" political backgrounds as defined by the criteria of that time. The situation was further complicated, however, by the redefinition of what constituted a worker or a peasant. Young people were—at least for purposes of college admissions—regarded as having been transformed by the mandatory post-secondary school work requirement. This redefinition of class was not strong enough to erase the stigma of a "bad" class or political family background. But it did effectively blur the urban/rural and sometimes the cadre/non-cadre distinction as well. Thus an urban senior secondary school graduate sent down to the countryside entered college as a rural, not an urban, youth. Educators insisted at that time, and still do, that all were regarded then as "peasants" and that the universities did not distinguish in admissions between youth born and reared in the countryside and those who had only resided there for a short time.

Today, all such considerations have been eliminated as criteria for admission to college. Nevertheless, after so many years of professed concern for worker-peasant admissions, university administrators remain on the defensive over the question of who is benefiting from the new enrollment policies. The reticence to release statistics on the social composition of college students is undoubtedly related to the internal controversy stirred by the new policies, which have removed the constraints both *against* youths from bad family backgrounds and *in favor* of those sectors of the population that have heretofore been the main beneficiaries of Communist rule.

That there is controversy was indicated clearly by the charge, made soon after the college entrance examinations were restored and before the leftist opposition had been effectively silenced, that the changing enrollment system would favor the offspring of the existing educated elite. More specifically, it was claimed that the restored entrance examinations and the new admissions criteria would ultimately lead to the favoring of urban areas over rural and of students from exploiting and intellectual families over those of workers and peasants.[2]

The official response to this challenge was to suggest that those presenting it were disgruntled cadres whose own children would be denied access to the easy "back-door" college admissions that the Cultural Revolution enrollment system facilitated. The statistical response was, however, a bland assertion that 87 percent of the 1977 freshman class nationwide were from the families of workers, peasants, soldiers, cadres, and intellectuals;[3] and that "over 99 percent" of the 1979 freshmen were of working-class origin.[4]

The most detailed national figures to appear to date outline a number of social criteria for the 1980 and 1981 candidates. These data were published in the *Guangming ribao*, 4 August 1981, and are translated in table 12 (p. 133). Unfortunately, they do not include statistics showing class background and have been deliberately designed to obscure the urban/rural distinction.

Following the lead suggested by the officially published statistics, university administrators exhibited a similar reluctance to specify the social or class composition of their student bodies. Those interviewed were often willing to comment in general terms, however. Said one: "Most people agree that the college entrance examinations are a good thing, but some do not. The proportion of intellectuals' children now getting into college is large, but workers' and peasants' children are few in number. So there has been some criticism of this."

Another estimated that about 60 percent of his university's freshmen were coming from keypoint middle schools. He noted further that most students from the rural areas had to be able to attend middle school in a prefectural or county town, since few were now qualifying for college from commune middle schools. The prevalence of county town middle school graduates among students of rural background was emphasized at another university as well. Administrators at yet a third institution also noted that "most" students in the key universities were now coming from keypoint middle schools and added that "most" were the children of intellectuals. This was because students from worker-peasant family backgrounds generally "could not achieve the high scores necessary to gain admission to the keypoint middle schools." The popular science specialties had similarly high proportions of urban students, since the large number of applicants in those fields had raised the passing scores beyond the levels that rural candidates as a whole were capable of achieving.

Among the schools visited, this trend was at its most advanced at Fudan University. Fudan reported that only "twenty-odd" of the 1,342 freshmen it admitted in 1980 were from the countryside (including by Fudan's reckoning, city suburbs, but *not* county towns). Also at Fudan, some 70 percent of the students were coming from keypoint middle schools.

Despite the obvious problem this question created for them, six universities and one branch campus did provide some statistical breakdowns on various social characteristics of their student bodies. These are presented in tables 13 through 19 (pp. 134-40). The figures provided by Jilin University, Jiangxi Gongda, People's University, and the Nankai University branch campus appear to be the most reliable.

The Jilin figures (table 13) are helpful in showing changes over time between 1976, the last year that students were enrolled under the Cultural Revolution recommendation system, and the years following the restoration of the entrance examinations. Administrators at this university selected for analysis four different classes *(ban)* of students, two in the sciences and two in liberal arts. These four classes had a combined enrollment of 182 (out of a total student body of 4,123) during the 1979-80 academic year. How and why these four classes were selected was not revealed, nor was any indication offered as to the representative nature of the sample.

Deliberate attempts to obfuscate in this area did occur. One university selected for analysis only the 1980 freshmen in one academic department, namely, Chinese language and literature. The result showed that of the 111 freshmen surveyed, 77 percent were of peasant origin, which was defined as households where agriculture *(nongye)* was the main source of income—whether located in a city suburb, county town, or rural village. The statistical breakdown presented for "family background" was as follows:

Cadre	7
Army	2
Intellectual	3
White collar	3
Worker	7
Small business	1
Urban poor	2
Peasants	86

It was later revealed inadvertently that the Chinese department was one of only three, all in the liberal arts, on that campus with large numbers of rural students. The other two departments were history and politics. "All or a majority" of the students in other departments were of urban origin. In 1980 this school had twelve academic departments with a total student body of approximately four thousand.

By contrast, the Jilin figures seem to duplicate the informal and impressionistic views most often advanced by university people, namely, that it is the children of intellectuals who are the main beneficiaries of the new admissions policies. Now that academic criteria have been allowed to assume their natural weight, it is said, the children of educated parents have regained the access to a college education that was previously denied them. Similarly, it is agreed that the losers are working-class youth and especially those from the rural areas.

In addition, however, the Jilin figures also show what university people all know but rarely talk about nowadays, namely, that the children of leadership cadres are continuing to gain admission to college. Many allegations have been made in recent years about how they benefited during the Cultural Revolution decade through influence-peddling and connections. But they appear to have survived the reinstitution of the college entrance exams with little untoward result. This suggests either that cadres' children perform better academically than the intellectuals evaluating them have been willing to give them credit for openly; or that the present admissions policies leave more scope for back-door manipulations than those promoting them will admit. In fact, as we have seen above, both groups are probably able to exploit the present system about equally to their own advantage. Hence the informal opinions expressed by university people about the academic performance of intellectuals' children, while not incorrect, nevertheless reflect the intellectuals' bias. This undoubtedly arises both from a sense of intellectual superiority and from the resentment caused by past discrimination suffered at the hands of these same cadres.

In the limited Jilin sample, students from cadre families more or less held their own over the period shown, ranging from 42.8 percent of the 1976 class to 36.5 percent of the 1979 class. By contrast, students from intellectual families rose from 9.5 percent in 1976 to 46.5 percent and 26.8 percent in the 1978 and 1979 classes, respectively. Worker-peasant youth (not including sent-down youth) declined from 42.8 percent in the 1976 class to 19.5 percent in the 1979 class.

With the exception of the Jilin figures, the statistics provided by the universities are not particularly helpful either in proving or in disproving the current conventional wisdom concerning the social background of the post-Cultural Revolution college students. Indeed, the more comprehensive but incomplete Wuhan University figures (table 14) actually show trends in the opposite direction, between 1977 and 1980. No figures were given for the class entering in 1976, nor was there any attempt to explain why those provided for the other years contained so many discrepancies. The Nanjing University figures (table 15) also show a large proportion of rural and working-class students among that school's 1980 freshmen.

It is now said that the Chinese People's University in Beijing remained closed throughout the 1966-76 decade because of the school's status as the main institution for training leadership cadres. Since these were the chief target of the Cultural Revolution, their school had to be attacked for both the symbolic and the substantive nature of its role as the premier institution responsible for producing them. They appear now to have resumed their position of dominance there, since their children comprised, at 41.7 percent, the single largest group within the student body (table 16). Only 4.6 percent were the offspring of intellectuals, while another 14.7 percent are from other white-collar families. The cadre "class," as some have critically referred to it, would indeed appear to be reproducing itself if the statistics provided here are accurate.

The Jiangxi Gong-da figures (table 17) are useful because, as noted, this university contains the "unpopular" agricultural specialties, and if the national enrollment regulations cited above are any indication, it is in such a school that the largest proportion of rural students is likely to be found. Similarly, Nankai University Branch School (table 18) shows a large proportion of students from worker families.

As might have been expected with the abolition of the post-secondary school work requirement, the average age of college freshmen is declining, a fact which is also related to the declining number of Party members among the new students. Eighteen is the minimum age for membership in the Communist

Party. The great majority of students are now entering college directly from middle school. The overwhelming preponderance of CYL members among them has already been mentioned.

The one unheralded trend that was both acknowledged everywhere informally and demonstrated clearly by the statistics provided—indicating that little controversy surrounds this issue—was the declining female enrollment since 1976. The figures showing this trend are reproduced in table 20 (p. 141), which does include some statistics for 1976.

Administrators at all universities cited the same basic facts: fewer women than men were taking the college entrance examinations; fewer women were achieving passing scores; and the number of women gaining admission to all the universities visited was declining. Nationwide, women constituted one-third of the candidates taking the college entrance examinations, as shown in table 12, and 24 percent of the total college population.[5]

While all universities denied that there were any enrollment quotas for women, two did speak of informal minimum demands although they did not say from where. Accordingly, women were to comprise not less than 20 percent of the student body at Wuhan University and 15 percent at Jiangxi Gong-da. The latter school had in fact set its own goal of 25 percent but was far from achieving it under the new enrollment system. During the Cultural Revolution decade, women had comprised "about one-third" of this university's enrollment. In 1980, only 7.6 percent of its new students were women, as shown in table 20.

Administrators at Lanzhou University (table 19) similarly claimed there was a stipulation that they should "try" to enroll more women. Nevertheless, they noted that "since we do not look down on women, we do not make any special exceptions for them; if they make the grade, then we can admit them." Unfortunately, their grades were simply not good enough, and so their numbers had declined from 26 percent of the freshman class at Lan-da in 1977 to 13 percent in 1979.

At Nanjing University, administrators claimed women were actually being given preference there within the ten-point range. But their ranks were dwindling nonetheless, and by 1980 they comprised only 20 percent of the total student body at Nan-da. The reason was that fewer women are now said to be applying for admission there.

Administrators offered two general explanations for the declining proportion of women among their students. One was the tradition of educating boys before girls, still said to be prevalent in the countryside. This tradition was cited as a significant influence on the sex ratios of students coming from the county towns and rural areas. But this could not explain the *declining* proportion of women entering college since 1976. That was more specifically attributed to the observed fact that girls do not do as well as boys in senior middle school. Hence, the restored academic criteria governing college admissions meant that girls of necessity lost out in the competition.

There are, of course, intervening considerations. The pressures from above to admit women students to college that were built into the pre-1976 recommendation system, together with the other social and political biases, have been withdrawn. One administrator at Nanjing University speculated further that women had a much clearer field of competition during the 1966-76 decade, when "no one wanted to go to college and become an intellectual." Intellectual families, at least, wanted their sons to seek employment in factories in order to promote the family's "political development." "The main thing then," he said, "was to try to change the political status of the family." And as we have seen, class status in China is passed on through the male line and is determined primarily by the occupation of the father. Now that the bias against intellectuals has been dropped and they have been officially designated as "part of the working class," families can once again pursue their "development" by sending their sons to college. It is within the context of this heightened competition that daughters are losing out to their brothers.

Whatever the intervening considerations, everyone agrees that women are losing out in the race for admission to college. Yet, more disturbing than the real decline in the proportion of women college students are the ready rationalizations provided for the phenomenon. Assumptions about the physical and intellectual inferiority of women are widely held in academic circles and are based on arguments of biological determinism that might have been acceptable a century ago but which sound quaint at best today.

The pattern was described by several administrators in the same terms. At the primary-school level, the girls' grades are better than those of the boys. The girls' superior performance is explained by a more diligent but "dead" *(si)* approach to their studies. The boys, by contrast, are more active and more alive *(huo)* intellectually at this age. These differences result in the gradual equalization of performance between the sexes in junior middle school, by the end of which the boys have overtaken the girls. Since girls at this age no longer test as well as boys, the entrance exams for senior secondary school restored in the late 1970s have resulted in the declining proportion of girls at that level and, consequently,, at the college level as well.

As to why the girls begin to fall behind in junior middle school, the Hainan Island schoolteacher interviewed in Hong Kong had volunteered cheerfully that it was because "girls' brains stop developing earlier than do those of boys." This statement was relegated to the status of "unverifiable opinion" until an administrator at Shanghai's East China Teachers' Training University said something similar. The most basic reason why girls fell behind in middle school, she said, was "physical." There was, unfortunately, not time for her to explain what it was about a girl's physique *(shenti)* that separated her from the boys at this age, since it was a "complex" problem. An all-male group of middle school administrators at the next stop came to the point very quickly, however. They asserted that men did better than women academically "because women's brains are, on the average, two hundred cubic centimeters smaller than those of men."

Similar reasoning also appeared in the explanation given by keypoint middle schools in Guangzhou for raising their admissions scores for girls by ten points: "After entering middle school, the intelligence *(zhili)* of girls does not develop as well as that of boys."[6] Nor, apparently, are such views confined to middle-school teachers and the universities which train them. Health Ministry personnel subsequently confirmed the general belief in the relationship between female intelligence and brain size in conversations with a foreign medical administrator.

Mao's old slogan that "women hold up half the universe" was apparently little more than a political invention imposed upon an unwilling and unbelieving audience; the latter seems now to be counterattacking with ammunition from its outdated arsenal of craniometry.[7] Perhaps Chinese women should be thankful that other more sophisticated rationalizations, influenced by more contemporary Western research in the field of developmental psychology, are also being used to explain their inferiority.[8]

Whatever the rationalizations, the assumption of female inferiority has been built into the enrollment regulations although administrators were unwilling to divulge the details. That there are, however, some sort of enrollment principles *limiting* the annual enrollment of women and that they are not always outperformed by men seems evident from remarks attributed in the press to a spokesman for the Beijing Enrollment Office in 1981. Among the problems complicating enrollment work in the capital that year, he noted, was that more women than men had achieved the minimum passing score (now called the *diaodang fenshuxian* in Beijing). "This," he said, "created a great contradiction with respect to the demand for the ratio between men and women students in college enrollment."[9]

Apparently, there is at least a "demand" that women college students should not exceed men in number, even if the former do score higher than the latter on the college entrance exams. Moreover, the Education Ministry spokesman claimed that women candidates now actually constitute 50 percent of the total number taking the college entrance examinations in the two main urban centers of Beijing and Shanghai.

Conclusions

The figures cited in this chapter, with the exception of those on female enrollments, can clearly not be regarded as definitive. But what they do suggest, together with the data on admissions criteria and the pattern of special preferences, is the reaffirmation of certain traditional divisions of labor that the Cultural Revolution and earlier enrollment policies sought to disrupt. Whether those pre-1976 efforts actually increased the access of workers and peasants to a college education remains to be proved. What those efforts did do, however, was to establish the objective as an official ideal. Their corollary was reduced access for the children of the intelligentsia. At present, with the constraints that worked against the latter and in favor of workers and peasants removed, the traditional divisions have reappeared, not only naturally, but because of positive encouragement as well.

This is indicated most clearly in the division of labor between the key schools and ordinary institutions. Where exceptions must be made for the "disadvantaged," it is primarily the local junior colleges that make them. The highest-scoring students are concentrated in the few best universities where few, if any, concessions of quality are granted to "underprivileged" candidates of any kind. Women are admitted in "appropriate" ratios and fields of study. National minorities and Overseas Chinese once again have institutions of their own with entrance requirements and curricula designed for their own cultural levels. Hence, exceptions need not be made for these groups in the key schools, although a few minority students are now apparently being admitted into carefully segregated classes. In similar vein, the enrollment regulations acknowledge the difficulty of filling quotas in unpopular fields of study. Enrollment is therefore to be concentrated within those same sectors, that is, among the children of parents already employed within them. There is once again a proper place for everyone, and everyone is being channeled into it.

The rationale underlying this traditional "streaming" by family origin and occupation which ensures that status is passed on from one generation to the next, can be seen in the comments of intellectuals sent to the countryside during the Cultural Revolution. For example, someone with a peculiarly slow manner of speech is not mentally or physically handicapped but "just a typical peasant." Others noted that "the peasants work like animals"; and that "a person must be born to that kind of life to be able to accept it."

The same view was illustrated in another way by a former medical college teacher interviewed in Hong Kong, who recalled that during enrollment they always looked for candidates from medical families since such students would have less difficulty adjusting to the sort of life demanded by the profession. The special preference offered to candidates whose families are already employed in certain unpopular fields is based on the same assumption.

During the Cultural Revolution and before, some of these traditional stratifications, divisions of labor, and social prejudices were attacked in the interests of something resembling *social* modernization. Expressed in terms of the socialist ideals of the period, the declared aim was to reduce differences between town and countryside and between mental and manual labor. Ironically, the conventional divisions are being reinforced today as the most efficient means of allocating scarce resources in the interests of *economic* modernization, to which the social goals have now been subordinated.

So firm is the commitment to this strategy at present that no effort is being made to counteract or even camouflage the aura of special privilege that has been re-created--particularly for the children of intellectuals—in the matter of access to schooling. As mentioned, the children of intellectuals are uniformly regarded as capable of performing better academically than others. This is the acknowledged reason for locating keypoint primary and middle schools in neighborhoods where intellectuals congregate and for giving their children preferential access to such schools. Similarly, it is the custom to find places in these schools for the children of the teachers who work in them. Finally, this logic has led to the provision of extra money to the keypoint universities for the expressed purpose of providing a better education for faculty members' children than they could otherwise expect to receive in the regular city school system, as will be described in the following chapter.

Even the argument of intellectual superiority, however, would not seem to justify such developments as the creation of a special night-school for the children of personnel at Fudan University who did not qualify for admission as regular students; or the preferential access (also described below) that Fudan children are granted, by reason of their parentage, to Fudan's affiliated middle school, which enjoys preferential access to the university itself.

In the long run, the promise of economic modernization will undoubtedly be realized in shrinking social differences as has been the case in the capitalist West. But even in the West, which currently represents for the Chinese the epitome of economic development, affirmative-action college admissions programs have been found to be socially desirable and hence politically expedient. One can only wonder, therefore, how long the Chinese Communists—with decades of rhetoric behind them and a political constituency based on an ideological appeal to workers and peasants—will be able to maintain the undiluted elitism inherent in the present education policies.

That the old ideals have not vanished with the political tide was demonstrated by the critique of keypoint schools that flared briefly in the press in late 1981. Despite the speedy suppression of the public debate, the criticism continues "in society" together with the conditions that inspired it. In refusing to modify the structure of the education system they have re-created since 1976, policy-makers remain unwilling to treat the criticism as legitimate. To date, they have only shown a willingness to acknowledge that the critique has a life of its own and is not just a political invention of the discredited radical pre-1976 leadership. This course of action appears to be politically unsound since it means abandoning an issue of acknowledged social concern to the opposition. But policy-makers seem to be gambling on the assumption that they have effectively destroyed that opposition and can successfully distract public attention from the issue with the lure of economic development.

CHAPTER VII

Trends for the Future

A wide range of complaints about the college entrance examinations and the new enrollment system were voiced by university administators. These were the complaints of the system's supporters rather than its detractors, however, and were not motivated by the larger political critique discussed in the preceding chapter. On the contrary, some of the universities' demands were aimed at pushing the system in an even more elitist direction. The complaints revolved essentially around two main issues. The first, raised specifically by the key schools, involved the familiar demands for greater university autonomy in admissions so as to "guarantee quality." A second more general complaint, not the immediate concern of the universities themselves, had to do with the administrative and financial burdens created by the ponderous national examinations system. Also present in the debate was the foreign criticism of the entrance examinations being used as the sole criterion for admission to college. Administrators anticipated that the debate then in progress on those issues would lead to significant changes in the enrollment system. As of late 1983, however, only a few of the possible changes being discussed in 1980 had materialized and the system remained essentially the same as it was at that time.

Among the changes designed to meet the universities' demands for more autonomy, some had actually just been approved in 1980 and were in the initial stages of implementation. Quota jumping and the linked middle schools preference scheme are two examples in this area. A related change that was being contemplated involved the transformation of some of the middle schools that are affiliated with the key universities *(fushu zhongxue)* into college preparatory schools. The "prep school" existed prior to the Cultural Revolution, and its restoration was being actively considered at Fudan in late 1980. That university's affiliated middle school was then in the process of being restored to it after having been administered by Shanghai's Yangpu district throughout the Cultural Revolution decade.

The affiliated middle school should not be confused with the linked *(guagou)* middle school described previously. The affiliated middle schools at teachers' training universities can and do serve as sites for practice teaching. But at other kinds of universities this is not the case and their affiliated middle schools serve very different functions. Prior to 1966, these functions essentially entailed offering college preparatory courses and/or educating the children of university personnel, since such schools are normally located on or adjacent to the campuses of the universities with which they are affiliated. These two functions were not necessarily synonymous. During the Cultural Revolution decade, the college preparatory role was eliminated and most, although not all, such schools were transferred to the administrative jurisdiction of the locality in question.

Now these schools are being returned to university administration and control. The nature of the administrative arrangements appears to vary depending on whether the school still serves primarily the university community or has been fully integrated into the city school system. Both Fudan's affiliated middle school and the Number Two Affiliated Middle School of the East China Teachers' Training University had recently been "returned" to those universities. But the universities were actually sharing administrative responsibilities with the city of Shanghai, since the two middle schools were among the most prestigious municipal keypoints enrolling students from throughout the city. Fudan's middle school was nevertheless giving "a little preference" to the children of university personnel. Two classes were reserved for them, and they were regarded as "commuter students" since all live nearby on the university campus. Other students live in school dormitories.

Where the affiliated middle schools had not been so integrated into the city school system, administration is being turned over entirely to the key universities. The financing for these middle and primary schools, which serve primarily faculty and staff children, is now allocated directly by the Ministry of Education and included within the universities' total budgets. The funds amount to more than is normally granted by the localities for ordinary schools at these levels. This discrepancy is explained as one of the legitimate privileges granted to the keypoint universities "so that in this way they can better run the middle schools for their own children."

Wuhan University's affiliated middle school, run by the university alone, was financed by the city government throughout the Cultural Revolution decade but otherwise remained under university administration. More recently, the Education Ministry began allocating directly to the university the funds to run its affiliated primary and middle schools. The funds are also more generous than the previous budgetary allocations for these schools by the city of Wuhan.

Now that this step has been taken, the next is to consider whether some of the affiliated schools might also have their college preparatory function restored to them. This would entail a curriculum more closely tailored to that of the university; extra materiel and equipment; a teaching staff bolstered by university faculty; and preferential admissions arrangements with the parent university for graduates. The main purpose of such a school would be to "guarantee quality" for the university by "controlling the origins" of the talent supplied to it. Prior to the Cultural Revolution, some 80 percent of the graduates from Fudan's college preparatory affiliated middle school were admitted to that university, and the remaining 20 percent had no difficulty obtaining admission to other universities.

The Fudan affiliated middle school and others like it were severely criticized for the caste-like nature of the education they provided, representing, as they did, not only intellectual excellence but intellectual elitism and special privilege as well. At Fudan, however, the restoration of the middle school's college preparatory status was being considered as one means of guaranteeing quality, which university administrators there and elsewhere said could not be maintained by the present national enrollment system alone. As of late 1980, the Ministry of Education had not yet given its approval for this move with respect to Fudan University's affiliated middle school. But the changes already sanctioned had already transformed it into something very close. Those changes were the restoration of the school's affiliated status with Fudan; and the preference in admission to the university granted to graduates of all Fudan's linked *(guagou)* middle schools, of which this just happens to be one.

Administrators at East China Teachers' Training University explained further that prior to the Cultural Revolution, the college entrance examinations were actually waived for students at its Number Two Affiliated Middle School. This was done on an "experimental basis" at several other universities as well before 1966. The universities were responsible for maintaining to their own specifications the curricula and standards of these schools and were permitted also to admit their graduates without requiring them to sit for the national college entrance examinations. But the universities could give the graduates of these schools a separate entrance exam. At the East China school, such an exam was given to its graduates as the only requirement for admission to the university.

Similar experimental arrangements were sanctioned in 1981, although the exact nature of their implementation is not known. The Ministry of Education called upon each province to consider allowing one or two schools therein to experiment with individual rather than unified enrollment, albeit still in accordance with candidates' scores on the national entrance examinations.[1] This appears to be similar to the development described most fully at Fudan, whereby the university has the right to give preference in admission to graduates from its own linked middle schools as long as those candidates have made the grade on the entrance exams.

In addition, independent enrollment was in effect by 1980 for special kinds of students and universities. These included Overseas Chinese and in 1981 the two schools established for them, Jinan University in Guangzhou and the Overseas Chinese University in Fujian, enrolled 270 students who applied directly to them without taking the national entrance examinations.[2] Fine arts and physical education institutes may also recruit independently.[3]

Other demands from the universities for more autonomy in enrollment have not been met, however. Thus some administrators spoke of a general objection on their part to the practice of enrolling on the basis of the candidate's total examination score. Some students, they declared, could be outstanding in one subject, and the university should be allowed to admit them on that basis alone without having to consider the total score, which could disqualify such a student. This complaint was apparently disregarded, since the new 1981 regulations actually fixed new rules requiring specific standards in the two basic subjects of math and Chinese language for candidates in both the sciences and the liberal arts.

As noted, the 1981 enrollment regulations also began requiring the universities to consider the candidate's all-around performance in middle school, including social activities and physical fitness. This is not likely to have met with much enthusiasm among the keypoint universities, at least, given their obvious desire to raise the academic qualifications of their students.

Everyone seemed to be aware of, if not in agreement with, the foreign critique of using entrance examination scores as the sole criterion for admission. The Education Ministry spokesman made specific reference to materials from the National Testing Service in Princeton, New Jersey, which explain that a student's capabilities cannot be adequately judged by a single examination score. Yet the key universities and the Education Ministry appeared somewhat at cross purposes in their approach to this issue. The universities were using it in their demands for greater autonomy from the constraints of the entrance examination scores (while nevertheless relying on that score even more heavily when it suited their purposes, as with the quota jumping scheme). But the Ministry, while giving in to other demands for autonomy, imposed additional general enrollment requirements which actually contradicted the universities' desire for the right to enroll students on the basis of single-subject performance alone.

Weighing perhaps more heavily than the problems reflected by the foreign critique of the entrance examinations, however, are the administrative and financial burdens associated with giving those examinations to far larger numbers of candidates than was ever necessary in the 1960s. Administrators were, in 1980, discussing a number of alternatives aimed at reducing these burdens in addition to the locally administered preliminary qualifying exams and all the other measures designed to reduce the numbers sitting for the national unified examinations.

One alternative mentioned by the Education Ministry spokesman was to abolish the national examinations and return to the method used in 1977, when the exams were unified only at the provincial level. Another possibility being contemplated, according to administrators at Zhongshan University, was to maintain the national entrance examinations but to use them as the main criterion for admission only to the national keypoint universities. Under this alternative, the small local schools with lower standards could simply give their own examinations since they enroll only local students in any case. At the same time, the 1960s experiment in waiving the national examinations for those graduating from the affiliated prep schools attached to key universities was also being reconsidered.

One administrator at Shandong University predicted that the national examinations would, once all the arguing was over, be retained but that major revisions would be introduced in the way students were enrolled. The only point that all agreed on was that "great changes" were in store. But as of late 1983, no such great changes had materialized. Having rejected the radical experiment in college enrollment attempted during the Cultural Revolution decade, present leaders set about restoring the pre-Cultural Revolution enrollment system immediately when they regained power in 1976. The unwieldly features of that system were rendered more so by the much larger number of candidates it was required to serve, leading to the 1980 debate over the need for reform. But having recreated the system in its pre-Cultural Revolution image, and being conservative by nature, education leaders appear loath to do more than nibble around the edges of the basic structure. They have, however, been reasonably effective in reducing the numbers of candidates taking the examinations.

Perhaps the last word on the matter, for an interim period of uncertain duration, was written by an anonymous commentator in *Renmin jiaoyu* in early 1981. He noted that the fundamental reforms in the college entrance examinations and enrollment system necessary to solve the many problems acknowledged to be inherent therein would have to await the successful completion of the extensive restructuring underway at the secondary school level.[4] In the meantime, according to a simultaneous statement from the Ministry of Education, "everyone thinks that enrollment on the basis of the unified college entrance examinations should be continued."[5]

TABLE 1

Selected College Enrollment Quotas by Province

Province and Population	*1977*	*1978*	*1979*	*1980*	*1981*
Anhui 48,030,000					10,000
Beijing 8,706,000			11,000	10,054	10,000
Fujian 24,800,000		10,000			10,140
Gansu 18,940,000			4,000		
Guangdong 56,810,000	10,100	12,000		11,000	10,336
Guangxi 34,700,000		9,043	7,448		
Hunan 52,230,000					12,260
Inner Mongolia 18,510,000	4,000	4,700			6,826
Jiangsu 58,930,000			15,000	16,030	15,700
Jilin 21,846,000		11,000	10,800		
Qinghai 3,720,000			1,800		
Shandong 72,310,000		16,900		16,691	
Shanghai 11,320,000		12,000			13,000
Sichuan 97,740,000		20,775	18,000		18,000
Tianjin 7,390,000				5,487	
Tibet 1,830,000	780				
Zhejiang 37,920,000		7,712		12,000	

Note: There is always a discrepancy between the predetermined enrollment plan and the actual number of students enrolled. For example, the planned enrollment figure for Beijing in 1980, as shown in the table, was 10,054, while the actual enrollment was 10,657. Similarly, Tianjin's planned figure that year was 5,487, but the actual number enrolled was 5,726. As a general rule, any figures announced before the end of August will reflect the plan, while those announced after will represent the actual numbers enrolled. The latter are usually greater than the former in accordance with the ruling which permits schools to enroll 1-3 percent in excess of their plans. But figures announced in August and September will usually not yet contain any "extra-quota" enrollments, that is, those carried out in accordance with local needs in excess of and separate from the national plan. Such enrollments are sometimes not completed until October or November.

Sources: The population figures in this table are all from *Zhongguo baike nianjian, 1980* [China encyclopedic yearbook, 1980] (Beijing and Shanghai, 1980). Anhui: *Zhongguo baike nianjian, 1980* (hereafter, *Nianjian),* p. 91; and Hefei radio, 8 June 1981, in SWB, FE/6751/BII/9, 17 June 1981. Beijing: *Nianjian,* p. 62; (1979) Xinhua-English, 29 August 1979, in SWB, FE/6232/BII/12, 29 September 1979; (1980) *Beijing ribao,* 29 August 1980; (1981) *Beijing ribao,* 27 August 1981. Fujian: *Nianjian,* p. 95; (1978) Fuzhou radio, 19 October 1978, in JPRS/72188/6 November 1978/PRC/465; (1981) *Fujian ribao,* 6 September 1981. Gansu: *Nianjian,* p. 79; and Lanzhou University interview file, p. 4. Guangdong: *Nianjian,* p. 104; (1977) *Wenhuibao* (Hong Kong), 11 March 1978; (1978) Guangzhou radio, 7 October 1978, in JPRS/72082/20 October 1978/PRC/462; (1980) Zhongshan University interview file, p. 23; (1981) *Guangzhou ribao,* 27 July 1981. Guangxi: *Nianjian,* p. 106; the figures for 1978 and 1979 are from a photograph of the enrollment plan for Guangxi posted on a wall, which was taken by John P. Burns in Yangsuo county, Guangxi, on 2 July 1979. Hunan: *Nianjian,* p. 103; and Changsha radio, 24 March 1981, in SWB, FE/6698/BII/4, 13 April 1981. Inner Mongolia: *Nianjian,* p. 70; (1977) Kyodo-English (Huhehot), 27 October 1977, in SWB, FE/5653/BII/2, 29 October 1977; (1978) Huhehot radio, 17 June 1978, in FBIS, 25 July 1978, p. K-4; (1981) Huhehot radio, 28 April 1981, in SWB, FE/6714/BII/4, 4 May 1981. Jiangsu: *Nianjian,* p. 87; (1979) Nanjing radio, 19 May 1979, in SWB, FE/6129/BII/9, 31 May 1979; (1980) *Xinhua ribao* (Nanjing), 18 September 1980; (1981) *Xinhua ribao,* 31 July 1981. Jilin: *Nianjian,* p. 74; (1978) Changchun radio, 15 July 1978, in SWB, FE/5875/BII, 27 July 1978; (1979) Jilin University interview file, p. 18. Qinghai: *Nianjian,* p. 82; and Xining radio, 7 June 1979, in SWB, FE/6141/BII/13, 14 June 1979. Shandong: *Nianjian,* p. 85; (1978) Jinan radio, 16 October 1978, in SWB, FE/5959/BII/16, 3 November 1978; (1980) Jinan radio, 12 September 1980, in SWB, FE/6539/BII/5, 3 October 1980. Shanghai: *Nianjian,* p. 64; (1978) Shanghai radio, 16 September 1978, in JPRS/71998/5 October 1978/PRC/460; (1981) *Wenhuibao* (Shanghai), 22 May 1981. Sichuan: *Nianjian,* p. 109; (1978) Chengdu radio, 26 October 1978, in SWB, FE/5962/BII/15, 7 November 1978; (1979) Chengdu Middle School Number Seven notes, p. 2; (1981) Chengdu radio, 28 March 1981, in SWB, FE/6698/BII/4, 13 April 1981. Tianjin:

Nianjian, p. 65; and *Tianjin ribao*, 6 September 1980. Tibet: *Nianjian*, p. 114; and Lhasa radio, 30 January 1978, in SWB, FE/5739/BII/7, 14 February 1978. Zhejiang: *Nianjian*, p. 89; (1978) Hangzhou radio, 15 October 1978, in FBIS, 1 November 1978, G-4; (1980) *Zhejiang ribao*, 1 August 1980.

TABLE 2

College Entrance Examinations: Candidates and Freshmen (including extra-quota enrollments)

Year	*Candidates*	*Freshmen*	*Freshmen as % of candidates*
1977	5,700,000[a]	278,000[a]	4.87
1978	6,000,000[b]	400,000[c]	6.66
1979	4,684,000[d]	275,000[d]	5.87
1980	3,600,000[e]	281,200[f]	7.81
1981	2,589,000[g]	285,000[h]	11.0

Sources: (a) *Renmin ribao*, 12 May 1978. (b) Xinhua-Chinese, 25 July 1978, in SWB, FE/5883/BII, 5 August 1978. (c) *Renmin ribao*, 28 June 1979. (d) *Zhongguo baike nianjian, 1980*, p. 538. (e) *Renmin jiaoyu*, no. 4 (1981), p. 28. (f) *Zhongguo jingji nianjian, 1981* (Beijing and Hong Kong, 1981), p. IV-205. (g) *Guangming ribao*, 4 August 1981. (h) *Guangming ribao*, 9 August 1981.

TABLE 3

Secondary School Enrollments, 1949-80

	General secondary		*Specialized secondary*			
			Professional		*Vocational/Agricultural*	
	Schools	*Students*	*Schools*	*Students*	*Schools*	*Students*
1949	—	1,260,000[a]	—	220,000[b]	—	—
1952	—	3,100,000[a]	—	—	—	—
1957	—	7,000,000[a]	—	—	—	—
1965	—	14,418,000[a]	—	—	—	—
1974	—	36,500,000[c]	—	—	—	—
1977	123,000[d]	58,280,000[d]	2,200[d]	799,000[d]	—	—
1977-78	—	68,900,000[e]	2,500[e]	880,000[f]	1,200[e] (in factories)	300,000[e] (in factories)
1978-79	—	65,480,000[f]	—			
1979	142,100[g]	59,050,000[h]	—	1,199,000[h]	31[g] (vocational)	—
1980	118,377[i]	55,081,000[j]	2,052 (technical)	761,300 (technical)	390 (vocational)	133,600 (vocational)
			1,017 (normal)	482,100 (normal)	2,924 (agricultural)	320,000 (agricultural)
			3,069[g]	1,243,400[g]	3,314[g]	453,600[g]

Note: These statistics should be treated as approximations only, since most official Chinese figures on school enrollments contain unexplained discrepancies. For example, the secondary school enrollment statistics given to the World Bank by the Chinese Education Ministry are not identical with those provided by other sources as shown here (*China: Socialist Economic Development*, Annex G: Education Sector [Washington, D.C.: The World Bank, 1 June 1981], p. 100). Another unexplained discrepancy is the 10 million difference in the figures given for primary school enrollment between May 1978 (150 million) and June 1979 (140 million). (See Suzanne Pepper, "Chinese Education after Mao," *The China Quarterly*, no. 81 [March 1980], p. 6.) For a good "self-criticism" of statistical reporting in China and an explanation which indicates that the discrepancies are sometimes deliberate, see Sun Yefang, "Jiaqiang tongji gongzuo, gaige tongji tizhi" [Strengthen statistical work, reform the statistical system], *Jingji guanli* [Economic management], no. 2 (1981), pp. 3-5.

Sources: (a) *Peking Review*, no. 5 (3 February 1978), pp. 16-17. (b) Xinhua-English (Beijing), 23 September 1979, in *Xinhua News Bulletin*, 24 September 1979. (c) Thomas P. Bernstein, *Up to the Mountains and Down to the Villages* (New Haven: Yale University Press, 1977), p. 46. (d) Pepper, "An Interview on Changes in Chinese Education after the 'Gang of Four,' " *The China Quarterly*, no. 72 (December 1977), pp. 815-16. (e) Clark Kerr et al., *Observations on the Relations Between Education and Work in the PRC* (Berkeley: The Carnegie Council on Policy Studies in Higher Education, 1978), p. 93. (f) *Renmin ribao*, 28 June 1979. (g) *Zhongguo jingji nianjian, 1981*, pp. IV-205, 206. (h) *Beijing Review*, no. 20 (19 May 1980), p. 22. (i) *Guangming ribao*, 1 October 1981. (j) *Beijing Review*, no. 20 (18 May 1980), pp. 18-19.

TABLE 4

College Freshmen and Senior Secondary Graduates

Year	*Senior secondary graduates*	*College freshmen*	*College freshmen as % of senior secondary graduates*
1949	61,000	31,000	50.8
1957	187,000	106,000	56.6
1965	360,000	164,000	45.5
1976	5,172,000	217,000	4.2
1979	7,265,000	275,000	3.8
1980	6,160,000	281,000	4.56

Sources: 1949-79 figures are from *Zhongguo baike nianjian, 1980*, p. 538. The 1980 figures were cited by Jiang Nanxiang in *Wenhuibao* (Hong Kong), 17 December 1981.

TABLE 5

Physical Examination Results

Locality	*Number taking physical*	*Failures (%)*	*Unconditional pass (%)*	*Conditional pass (%)*
Jiangsu province (1980)	20,000	1.0	43.6	55.4
Fujian province (1980)	10,000	0.5	—	—
Shanghai (1980)	233,000	1.76	30.85	67.38
Beijing Western district (Xichengqu) (1979)	1,623	0.2	43.9	55.9

Sources: Jiangsu and Fujian: *Renmin jiaoyu*, no. 3 (1981), p. 10. Shanghai: *Wenhuibao* (Shanghai), 16 August 1980. Beijing: *Guangming ribao*, 7 December 1979. The Shanghai source notes that the failures there were due primarily to hepatitis, tuberculosis, and heart problems. The conditional passes can also be broken down further: in Jiangsu, 63.6% were reportedly myopic and 21% had a height or weight deficiency; in Fujian, 36% were myopic and 38% had a height or weight deficiency; in Shanghai, a "majority" of the conditional passes were myopic; and in Beijing, 78.6% were myopic and 16% had a height or weight deficiency.

TABLE 6

Selected Local Minimum Passing Scores, 1981

	Jiangsu	*Nanjing*	*Zhejiang*	*Shandong*	*Tianjin*	*Guangdong*
Non-key colleges						
Sciences	425	—	422	400	384	386
Liberal arts	395	—	393	360	358	360
Foreign languages	371	—	330	350	353	356
Physical education	250	—	180	—	—	160-180
Junior colleges						
Sciences	—	380	394	—	—	—
Liberal arts	—	325	368	—	—	—
Physical education	—	—	170	—	—	—
Factory and enterprise universities	—	—	—	—	371	—

Sources: Jiangsu: Xinhua ribao, (Nanjing), 31 July and 2 August 1981. Nanjing: *Xinhua ribao* (Nanjing), 18 August 1981. Zhejiang: *Zhejiang ribao*, 1 August 1981. Shandong: *Dazhong ribao* (Jinan), 2 August 1981. Tianjin: *Tianjin ribao*, 30 July 1981. Guangdong: *Guangzhou ribao*, 29 July 1981.

TABLE 7

Selected 1980 Local Minimum Passing Scores for Key Schools (with contrasting local mps for non-key schools in brackets)

Jurisdiction	*Sciences mps (points)*		*Liberal arts mps (points)*	
National[a]	360		330	
Tianjin	400	[360][b]	380	[303][b]
Shanghai	400		350	
Beijing	370		340	
Jiangsu	387[c]	[364][d]	365[c]	[336][d]
Jiangxi	373			
Zhejiang		[374][e]		[365][e]

Sources: The mps were revealed in the interviews, with the following exceptions: (a) *Guangming ribao*, 5 August 1980; (b) *Tianjin ribao*, 3 August 1980; (c) *Xinhua ribao* (Nanjing), 26 August 1980; (d) *Xinhua ribao* (Nanjing), 1 August 1980; and (e) *Zhejiang ribao*, 1 August 1980.

TABLE 8

Institutional Preferences of Freshmen Enrolling in Jiangxi Communist Labor University and Shandong University

	Jiangxi Gong-da 1980		*Shandong University 1979*	*Shandong University 1980*
	Number	*% of total*	*% of total*	*% of total*
First preference	215	32.72	68.7	80.8
Second preference	93	14.15	21.3	12.9
Third preference	44	6.69	4.4	3.0
Fourth preference	28	4.26	5.6*	3.3*
Fifth preference	91	13.85	—	—
Arbitrary assignment	186	28.31	—	—
TOTAL NUMBER	657		1,100 (approx.)	1,100 (approx.)

*Fourth preference and below.

Sources: Jiangxi Communist Labor University file, p. 36; and Shandong University file, p. 15.

TABLE 9

Range of Freshman Examination Scores

Jilin University: 1979 freshmen

Scores	Number of students	% of total
381-400	21	2.31
360-380	192	21.19
341-360	424	46.79
320-340	201	22.18
310-320	67	7.39
281-300	1	
TOTAL	906	

1979 national key university mps: sciences, 300; liberal arts, 310. 1979 Jilin provincial non-key mps: sciences, 270; liberal arts, 290; foreign languages, 250.

Jiangxi Communist Labor University: 1980 freshmen

Scores	Number of students	% of total
390-399	6	0.91
380-389	27	4.10
370-379	84	12.78
360-369	267	40.63
355-359	273	41.55
TOTAL	657	

1980 national key university mps: sciences, 360. 1980 Jiangxi provincial key mps: sciences, 373.

Sources: Jilin University file, p. 19; and Jiangxi Communist Labor University file, p. 36.

TABLE 10

National Expanded Enrollments

Year	*Extra-quota freshmen*	*Total freshmen enrolled*
1977 (entered spring 1978)[a]	60,000	278,000
1978 (entered fall 1978)[b]	107,000	400,000
1979[c]	?	275,000
1980[d]	7,400	281,200

AY 1980-81	*Total extra-quota students in school*	*Total students in school*
National[d]	112,800	1,143,700
Shanghai[e]	15,000	
Beijing[f]	17,440	

Note: As usual, the figures contain unexplained discrepancies: the total number of all extra-quota freshmen as shown from 1977-80 above is 174,400. But the total number of extra-quota students in school was given as 112,800 during the 1980-81 academic year, and the number of such students graduating in 1980 was only 3,100 *(Zhongguo jingji nianjian, 1981)*, p. IV-205). Since attrition rates are by all accounts extremely low at the tertiary level, the discrepancy, if not an error, may simply reflect confusion over status; several universities reported having allowed their 1978 commuter students to move on campus as room became available.

Sources: (a) Xinhua-Chinese (Beijing), 11 May 1978, in FBIS, 17 May 1978, p. E-6. (b) "Communiqué of the State Statistical Bureau," Xinhua-English (Beijing), 27 June 1979, in *Xinhua News Bulletin*, 28 June 1979. (c) *Zhongguo baike nianjian, 1980*, p. 538. (d) *Zhongguo jingji nianjian, 1981*, p. IV-205. (e) *Guangming ribao*, 3 December 1980. (f) *Guangming ribao*, 14 June 1980.

TABLE 11

Commuter Courses and Branch Campuses:
Numbers of Students and Enrollment Scores

School (program)	*Number of students enrolled*	*Year enrolled*	*Mps*	*Comparative mps*
Nankai University Branch (commuter)	998	1978	255 (sciences)	340[a]
Wuhan University (3-yr. tuition commuter course)	140	1980	320 (sciences) 300 (lib. arts)	400[b] (sciences) 380[b] (lib. arts)
Nanjing University (3-yr. commuter course)	671	1978	—	—
Zhongshan University (2-yr. tuition commuter course)	200	1980	—	—
Shandong University (3-yr. tuition commuter course)	132	1980	345 (sciences) 290 (lib. arts)	400[c] (sciences) 360[c] (lib. arts)
Shandong University (3-yr. commuter course for lab technicians)	123	1978	—	—
East China Teachers' Training University Branch (3-yr. technical course)	800	1979 & 1980 (combined)	360 (sciences)	400[d] (sciences)
Fudan University (tuition night-school for commuters)	249	1980	350	420[e] (sciences) 350[e] (lib. arts)
Hangzhou city (tuition commuter courses)		1980	320 (sciences) 310 (lib. arts)	374[f] (sciences) 365[f] (lib. arts)
and	720 (combined)			
Ningpo city (tuition commuter courses)		1980	330 (sciences) 280 (for. lang.)	360[g] (sciences) 345[g] (lib. arts)

Sources: Hangzhou and Ningpo figures are from *Zhejiang ribao*, 1 August and 18 September 1980; all others are from the interview files of the universities cited. The comparative mps used are the following: (a) national keypoint; (b) Wuhan University; (c) Shandong University (mps for home-province candidates); (d) Shanghai keypoint (both mps for 1980 only); (e) Fudan University; (f) Zhejiang provincial non-keypoint; and (g) Zhejiang provincial junior college.

TABLE 12

Profiles of the 1980 and 1981 College Candidates

	1981		*1980*
	Number	*% of total*	*% of total*
Sex			
Male	1,710,000	66.3	65.1
Female	870,000	33.7	34.9
Field of study			
Sciences	1,830,000	70.9	66.8
Liberal arts	680,000	26.4	33.2
Fine arts and physical education	66,000	2.6	—
Status/origin			
Current year middle school graduate (urban)	640,000	24.9	20.3
Current year middle school graduate (county town and village)	1,140,000	44.3	50.1
Urban youth sent down to the countryside and rural youth returned to the village	460,000	17.8	17.2
Employed worker and cadre; demobilized army personnel	60,000	2.4	3.4
Other (presumably, unemployed or "social" youth)	270,000	10.5	8.7
National minorities	139,000	5.38	5.2
Overseas Chinese, Hong Kong, Macao, Taiwan	2,240	0.08	0.05
TOTAL CANDIDATES	2,589,000		

Source: Guangming ribao, 4 August 1981.

TABLE 13

Social Composition of Jilin University Students
(number of students)

	Class A (1976)	*Class B (1977)*	*Class C (1978)*	*Class D (1979)*
Family background				
Cadre	18	24	16	15
Army	1	4	0	3
White collar	1	3	2	4
Intellectual	4	7	20	11
Worker	11	9	5	6
Peasant	7	9	0	2
	42	56	43	41
Urban/rural origin				
City	19	23	38	31
Countryside	20	27	5	9
Army	3	6	0	1
	42	56	43	41
Student's own status				
Current year middle school graduate	?	2	33	19
Sent-down youth	9	20	5	10
Cadre	5	6	2	1
White collar	?	1	0	0
Army	3	6	0	1
Worker	7	18	3	10
Peasant	8	3	0	0
	incomplete	56	43	41

Class A: 42 students in computer systems; enrolled in 1976.
Class B: 56 students in history; enrolled in 1977.
Class C: 43 students in computer software; enrolled in 1978.
Class D: 41 students in Japanese; enrolled in 1979.

Source: Jilin University file, pp. 48-49.

TABLE 14

Social Composition of Wuhan University Freshmen*
(number of students)

	1977	*1978*	*1980*
Family background (father's occupation)			
Leading cadre	85	158	155
Army	40	63	48
White collar	186	249	194
Intellectual	254	102	148
Worker	123	200	276
Peasant	348	244	380
Urban/rural origin			
City and county town	571	784	712
Suburbs	42	53	89
Village	492	195	413
Student's own status			
Current year middle school graduate	97	461	1,093
Sent-down youth	298	114	45
Worker, cadre, and white collar (employed)	512	228	—
White collar (employed)	—	—	20
Political status			
CYL member	903	728	1,119
CCP member	163	55	1
Other			
National minorities	16	10	19
Overseas Chinese	1	0	2
Average age (in years)	20.2	19.9	17.1
TOTAL FRESHMAN ENROLLMENT	1,204	1,001	1,214

*These figures should be treated with caution since only one set, the urban/rural origin for 1980, actually adds up to the stated total for the freshman class of the year in question. The category "social youth," or unemployed, is absent from the student's status set and might account for the gap there. The apparent discrepancies between the number of "peasant" background students and those originating in villages, suburbs, and county towns also needs explaining.

Source: Wuhan University file, pp. 67–70.

TABLE 15

Social Composition of Nanjing University Freshmen, 1980
(% of freshmen students)

Family background (father's occupation)	
Cadre, white collar, and intellectual	38.0
Worker, poor and lower-middle peasant	49.5
Other laboring people	12.5
Urban/rural origin	
City	38.3
Suburbs	14.0
Village	42.0
County town	5.0
Student's own status	
Current year middle school graduate	77.9
Sent-down youth	0.3
Worker	0.8
Cadre	0.0
Army	0.0
Other (presumably, older middle school graduates or social youth)	20.0
Political status	
CYL member	89.3
CCP member	0.0
Other	
National minorities	0.51
Overseas Chinese	0.0
Average age (in years)	18.0
TOTAL NUMBER OF STUDENTS	1,300 (approx.)

Source: Nanjing University file, pp. 6, 80.

TABLE 16

Social Composition of the Student Body of Chinese People's University, Spring 1980

Family background	*Number of students*	*% of total*
Cadre	821	41.67
White collar *(zhiyuan)*	289	14.67
Teacher *(jiaoyuan)*	91	4.61
Worker	244	12.38
Poor and lower-middle peasant	383	19.44
Other laboring people	88	4.46
Exploiting classes	15	0.76
Other	39	1.97
TOTAL STUDENT BODY	1,970	
Undergraduates	1,728	
Graduate students	242	

Source: Chinese People's University file, p. 6.

TABLE 17

Social Composition of Jiangxi Communist Labor University Freshmen, 1980

	Number of students	*% of total*
Family background		
Cadre, army, and white collar	90	13.69
Worker, poor and lower-middle peasant	420	63.92
Other	147	22.37
Student's own status		
Current year middle school graduate (urban)	80	12.17
Current year middle school graduate (county town & village)	370	56.31
Sent-down youth (urban origin)	21	3.19
Returned-to-village youth (rural origin)	85	12.93
Worker	2	0.30
Army	1	0.15
Others (e.g., awaiting employment)	98	14.91
Political status		
CYL member	535	81.43
CCP member	1	0.15
Average age (in years)	17	
TOTAL FRESHMEN	657	

Source: Jiangxi Communist Labor University file, p. 40.

TABLE 18

Social Composition of Nankai University Branch Campus
(commuter student body, all enrolled in 1978)

Family background	*% of total*
Cadre	27
Army	4
White collar	18
Intellectual	9
Worker	40
Peasant	6
Student's own status	*Number of students*
Current year middle school graduate	541
Sent-down youth	115
Worker	316
Peasant	5
Social youth	21
Urban/rural origin	*Number of students*
City	758
Countryside	240
TOTAL STUDENT BODY	998

Source: Nankai University file, p. 16.

TABLE 19

Characteristics of Lanzhou University Freshmen*

	1976	*1977*	*1978*	*1979*
Number of freshmen	845	---	---	1,000 (approx.)
Student's own status				
(% of freshmen)				
Current year middle school graduate	---	14.6	40.2	69.8
Sent-down youth	23.9	14.6	10.6	15.3
Worker	52.0	31.1	23.3	4.7
Army	4.5	0.5	0.5	0.6
White collar and nonmanual worker	20.8	40.0	22.5	1.9
Political status				
(% of freshmen)				
CYL member	70.	72.	75.	80.
CCP member	30.	14.	5.	1.
National minorities				
Number of students	32	27	12	14
% of freshmen	3.78	---	---	1.3
Average age (in years)	---	23	20	18

*An unanswered question concerning these figures arises from the total absence of peasant students. This is especially surprising since other data presented by this university showed 73% of the 1979 freshmen to be "from the countryside," while 66% that same year were of "peasant" family origin—referring to the family status three years prior to Liberation in 1949. No plausible explanation was offered to explain the apparent discrepancy.

Source: Lanzhou University file, pp. 4-6.

TABLE 20

Female Freshman Enrollments

School	*1976*	*1977*	*1978*	*1979*	*1980*
Jilin University					
Number	396	365	307	206	---
% of total	*39.91*	*28.89*	*21.85*	*22.53*	—
Wuhan University					
Number	406	335	183	167	316
% of total	*36.80*	*27.82*	*18.28*	*18.09*	*26.02*
Nanjing University					
Number	221	174	218	222	---
% of total	*31.61*	*19.61*	*16.16*	*19.57*	---
Lanzhou University					
Number	---	224	?	146	---
% of total	---	*26.0*	*18.0*	*13.34*	---
Jianxi Gong-da					
Number	---	---	---	---	50
% of total	*33**	---	---	---	*7.6*

*Approximate.

Sources: Jilin University file, p. 41; Wuhan University file, p. 67; Nanjing University file, p. 6; Lanzhou University file, p. 5; and Jiangxi Gong-da file, p. 39.

TEXT NOTES

Preface

1. The first report, on administrative reforms, appeared in *Modern China* 8, no. 2 (April 1982):147-204.
2. Xinhua-English, 16 September 1979, in SWB, FE/6232/BII/12, 29 September 1979.
3. The individual university loans were made primarily for the purchase of scientific equipment. The list of universities and the disciplines proposed for World Bank assistance were published in *China Trader: Weekly Bulletin* (Hong Kong), 9-15 August 1981.

Introduction

1. For these latter two announcements, see "Resolutions of the Eleventh National Congress," *Peking Review*, no. 35 (26 August 1977), p. 58; and *Guangming ribao*, 21 October 1977. Several books have recently been published on different aspects of Chinese education during the 1966-76 decade and the years immediately preceding. See: Theodore Hsi-en Chen, *Chinese Education since 1949* (New York: Pergamon Press, 1981); Stanley Rosen, *Red Guard Factionalism* (Boulder, Colo.: Westview Press, 1982); Susan L. Shirk, *Competitive Comrades* (Berkeley: University of California Press, 1982); Robert Taylor, *China's Intellectual Dilemma* (Vancouver: University of British Columbia Press, 1981); and Jonathan Unger, *Education under Mao* (New York: Columbia University Press, 1982).
2. Xinhua-English, 14 September 1979, in SWB, FE/6232/BII/12, 29 September 1979.
3. Interview files: Shandong, p. 19; Nanjing, p. 83; Zhongshan, pp. 19-20; Fudan, pp. 53, 55.
4. Interview files: Nankai, p. 10; Fudan, p. 55; Jilin, p. 16; Shandong, p. 9.
5. *Zhejiang ribao*, 8 July 1981.
6. *Guangming ribao*, 18 and 27 May 1979.
7. The general eligibility requirements are widely publicized in the national and local press; see, for example, *Guangming ribao*, 16 March 1981; *Nanfang ribao*, 27 March 1981 and 11 May 1980; and *Beijing ribao*, 15 May 1981 and 17 May 1980. They are also printed in the *State Council Bulletin*, no. 4 (25 April 1981), pp. 118-19, and no. 5 (23 June 1980), pp. 161-62.
8. *Guangming ribao*, 13 July 1981; *Wenhuibao* (Shanghai), 17 March 1981; *Beijing ribao*, 17 March 1981; "Renzhen zhuahao gaozhong biyebande gongzuo: qiantan gaokao yuxuan" [Conscientiously grasp the work of the senior middle school graduating classes: a brief discussion of the preliminary selection for the college entrance examinations], *Renmin jiaoyu*, no. 4 (1981), pp. 28-29; and "Yijiubalingnian gaodeng xuexiao zhaosheng gongzuode guiding" [1980 college enrollment work regulations], *State Council Bulletin*, no. 5 (23 June 1980), p. 162.

Chapter I

1. Xinhua-English (Beijing), 17 August 1979, in *Xinhua News Bulletin*, 18 August 1979.

2. Suzanne Pepper, "Chinese Education after Mao," *The China Quarterly*, no. 81 (March 1980), p. 6; *Zhongguo jingji nianjian, 1981* [China economic yearbook, 1981], (Beijing and Hong Kong, 1981), p. IV-205.
3. The declining numbers are recorded in *Zhongguo jingji nianjian, 1981*, p. IV-206; and *Beijing Review*, no. 20 (1980), p. 22, and no. 20 (1981), pp. 18-19. They do not match exactly the total official enrollment figures as issued by the State Statistical Bureau that are shown in table 3.
4. *Yangcheng wanbao*, 13 July 1981; *Guangzhou ribao*, 11 August 1981.
5. Nanjing middle school notes, p. 3; Xiamen middle school notes, p. 11; *Fujian ribao*, 8 August 1981.
6. Jinan middle school notes, p. 12.
7. Shanghai affiliated middle school notes, pp. 4-5; *Wenhuibao* (Shanghai), 21 October 1981, p. 4. On the small size of Shanghai's secondary school age cohort, see *Wenhuibao* (Shanghai), 25 February 1982.
8. *Beijing ribao*, 11 March 1981.
9. *Renmin ribao*, 12 November 1981.
10. *Beijing ribao*, 11 March 1981; *Guangzhou ribao*, 13 May and 11 August 1981.
11. *Xinhua ribao* (Nanjing), 15 and 17 August 1980.
12. Liaoningsheng jiaoyuju, "Juban gezhongmenleide zhongdeng zhiye jiaoyu" [Run various kinds of secondary vocational education], *Renmin jiaoyu*, no. 7 (1979), p. 45; Shenyang radio, 27 September 1980, in SWB, FE/6539/BII/5, 3 October 1980; *Guangming ribao*, 18 March 1981.
13. See, for example, Xining, Qinghai radio, 8 January 1981, in SWB, FE/6625/BII/14, 17 January 1981; *Zhongguo qingnian bao*, 9 May 1981; *Guangming ribao*, 5 October 1981; *Guangzhou ribao*, 4 August 1981.
14. Premier Zhao Ziyang acknowledged this problem in his report to the Fourth Session of the Fifth National People's Congress in late 1981 (Xinhua-English [Beijing], 14 December 1981, in *Xinhua News Bulletin*, 15 December 1981, p. 33).
15. Suzanne Pepper, "An Interview on Changes in Chinese Education after the 'Gang of Four.' " *The China Quarterly*, no. 72 (December 1977), p. 815; Jiang Nanxiang and Zhang Chengxian, "Kefu zuoqing sixiang yingxiang, gaohao jiaoyu diaozheng" [Overcome the influence of leftist thinking, readjust education well], *Hongqi*, no. 3 (1981), p. 28.
16. *Renmin ribao*, 11 August 1979.
17. Song Jian, "Population and Education," *Ziran bianzhenfa tongxun* [Journal of the Dialectics of Nature] (Beijing), no. 3 (June 1980), pp. 1-3; in JPRS/77745/China/PSM/178, 3 April 1981, p. 43.
18. *Renmin ribao*, 15 November 1981.
19. Chinese school administrators distinguish the professional schools as offering instruction of a higher level than that of vocational schools. As a simple rule of thumb, it is said that the students of the former become cadres *(ganbu)* upon graduation. Vocational schools, by contrast, produce skilled workers *(jishu gongren)*.
20. Xinhua-English (Beijing), 17 August 1979, in *Xinhua News Bulletin*, 18 August 1979; *Guangming ribao*, 20 May and 16 August 1979; Liaoningsheng jiaoyuju, "Run Various Kinds of Secondary Vocational Education," pp. 44-46; *Xinhua ribao* (Nanjing), 14 August 1980; *Guangzhou ribao*, 13 May 1981.
21. Shanghai Machine Building School notes, p. 7.
22. Xiamen Middle School Number Eight notes, p. 15, and Xinhua-English (Beijing), 26 October 1981, in FBIS, 28 October 1981, p. 0-1. The population of Xiamen city is approximately 200,000, with an additional 500,000 in the suburban areas. The combined urban and suburban population of Shanghai is 11 million.

23. *Dazhong ribao*, 21 August 1981.
24. This report is reprinted in *State Council Bulletin*, no. 16 (1 December 1980), p. 493.
25. *Guangming ribao*, 21 July 1980.
26. Nanjing affiliated middle school notes, p. 6.
27. Shanghai Bureau of Higher Education notes, p. 2; Jinan middle school notes, p. 2; Lanzhou middle school notes, p. 5.
28. Jinan, Shandong radio, 2 January 1981, in SWB, FE/6625/BII/14, 17 January 1981.
29. *Guangming ribao*, 5 August 1980 and 8 November 1979.
30. *Guangming ribao*, 21 July 1980, and *Wenhuibao* (Shanghai), 5 October 1980.
31. The reports cited are from the following sources, respectively: *Beijing ribao*, 11 November 1980 and 26 March 1981; *Nanfang ribao*, 12 November 1980; (for Sichuan) *Guangming ribao*, 2 October 1980; (for Guizhou) *Guangming ribao*, 7 July 1980; Jinan, Shandong radio, 2 January 1981, in SWB, FE/6625/BII/14, 17 January 1981; (for Fujian) *Guangming ribao*, 15 December 1980.
32. From an unpublished paper by Ruth Hayhoe, "China's Keypoint Mentality," p. 4.
33. For some examples of this, see Suzanne Pepper, "Education and Revolution," *Asian Survey* 18, no. 9 (September 1978):863-64.
34. *Zhongguo qingnian bao*, 21 November 1981.
35. *Wenhuibao* (Shanghai), 21 October 1981.
36. Both in *Zhongguo qingnian bao*, 12 December 1981. For other critical commentary, see *Zhongguo qingnian bao*, 31 October and 5 December 1981; *Guangming ribao*, 16 November and 5 December 1981; *Wenhuibao* (Shanghai), 12 December 1981; and *Beijing ribao*, 12 December 1981.
37. Only Shanghai's decision was actually reported in the Chinese press, however; see *Guangming ribao*, 7 November 1981. See also *International Herald Tribune*, New York Times Service (Shanghai), 21 December 1981.
38. *Beijing ribao*, 25 December 1981. Also in line with this argument, see *Renmin ribao*, 12, 15, and 17 November 1981.
39. *Guangming ribao*, 6 November 1981. For a few of the many articles either criticizing or announcing the abolition of streaming, see *Guangming ribao*, 31 October and 1, 4, 7, 12, and 26 November 1981.

Chapter II

1. Jilin University file, p. 22; *Guangming ribao*, 16 October 1979; *Beijing ribao*, 19 August 1980; *Zhongguo qingnian bao*, 11 September 1980.
2. Chengdu middle school notes, p. 2.
3. The Education Ministry's *Review Outline* for 1978 is translated and analyzed in *The 1978 National College Entrance Examination in the People's Republic of China*, ed. Robert D. Barendsen (Washington, D.C.: U.S. Department of Health, Education, and Welfare, 1979), pp. 11-56.
4. See, for example, *Guangming ribao*, 13 October 1981, 26 May and 6 April 1979, and 7 December 1978; *Wenhuibao* (Shanghai), 4 June, 24 April, and 27 March 1979.
5. *Wenhuibao* (Hong Kong), 10 November 1978; and Fuzhou, Fujian radio, 19 October 1978, in JPRS/72188/PRC/465, 6 November 1978, p. 36.
6. Nanchang, Jiangxi radio, 6 September and 16 August 1978, in FBIS, 8 September 1978, p. G-2, and 18 August 1978, p. G-2, respectively; *Wenhuibao* (Hong Kong), 21 December 1978, and Guangzhou radio, 7 October 1978, in JPRS/72082/20 October 1978/PRC/462, p. 68.

7. *Guangming ribao*, 30 September 1978.
8. *Fujiansheng jiaoyuju*, "Wei 'gaokao hongqi' huifu mingyu" [Restoring the reputation of the "red flag for the college entrance examinations"], *Renmin jiaoyu*, no. 1 (1979), pp. 35-37.
9. On that initial outburst, see Suzanne Pepper, "Chinese Education after Mao," *The China Quarterly*, no. 81 (March 1980), p. 63.
10. *Guangming ribao*, 30 September 1978; and 12 May, 5 and 16 June 1978.
11. *Guangming ribao*, 16 October 1979; *Zhongguo qingnian bao*, 2 August 1979; *Wenhuibao* (Shanghai), 12 June 1979.
12. See, for example, *Guangming ribao*, 23 January 1980; *Zhongguo qingnian bao*, 11 September 1980.
13. *Guangming ribao*, 5 August 1980.
14. Li Shuxi and Chen Hao, "Yijiubayinian gaokao shitide chansheng" [The development of the 1981 college entrance exam questions], *Renmin jiaoyu*, no. 8 (1981), pp. 39, 41.
15. East China Teachers' Training University file, p. 37.
16. *Guangming ribao*, 5 November 1981.
17. *Wenhuibao* (Shanghai), 19 November 1981.
18. *Guangming ribao*, 13 May 1981.
19. *Guangming ribao*, 11 May 1981.
20. *Beijing ribao*, 9 October 1981; and *Guangming ribao*, 27 January, 5 and 14 November 1981.
21. *Wenhuibao* (Hong Kong), 17 December 1981, or *Beijing ribao*, 3 January 1982. Jiang Nanxiang was replaced, along with many other central government ministers, in May 1982. The new minister of education is He Dongchang. For another discussion of some points in this section, see Stanley Rosen, "Obstacles to Educational Reform in China," *Modern China* 8, no. 1 (January 1982):3-40.

Chapter III

1. Jilin University file, p. 17.
2. Nanjing University file, pp. 78-79; *Xinhua ribao* (Nanjing), 2 August 1980 and 9 July 1981.
3. Shandong University file, pp. 8-9, 11.
4. *Nanfang ribao*, 27 March 1981.
5. The discussion of the contents of the application form is based primarily on the following interview files: Fudan, p. 50; Wuhan, pp. 61-62; Nanjing, pp. 75, 79; Lanzhou, p. 6; and also on *Zhongguo qingnian bao*, 11 October 1981; *Zhejiang ribao*, 18 September 1980, and *Banyuetan* [Fortnightly talks], no. 17 (1981), pp. 24-25.
6. On this last point, see also "Yijiubayinian gaodeng xuexiao zhaosheng gongzuode guiding," [1981 college enrollment work regulations], *State Council Bulletin*, no. 4 (25 April 1981), pp. 120-21.
7. These criteria were confirmed at all five universities where administrators were willing to discuss this question. Perhaps reflecting the renewed emphasis on politics that was registered in a number of areas in 1981, a stricter sounding interpretation of the personal traits which may disqualify a candidate for admission to college than that reported to me appeared in Zhao Sheng, "Jiu jinnian gaodeng xuexiao zhaosheng da duzhe wen" [Answering readers' questions on this year's enrollment to institutions of higher learning], *Renmin jiaoyu*, no. 3 (1981), p. 9.
8. *Wenhuibao* (Shanghai), 21 August 1980.
9. *Zhongguo qingnian bao*, 5 August 1980.

10. "1981 College Enrollment Work Regulations," and "Jiaoyubu guanyu yijiubayinian quanguo gaodeng xuexiao zhaosheng gongzuo huiyide baogao" [The Ministry of Education's report on the 1981 national college enrollment work conference], both in *State Council Bulletin,* no. 4 (25 April 1981), pp. 120 and 117, respectively.

11. *Renmin ribao,* 26 April 1978.

12. Also, *Guangming ribao,* 9 August 1979.

13. From interview files for Fudan (p. 50), Wuhan (p. 57), and Shandong (p. 13), and interpreted with the assistance of Prof. Peter Lisowski, Department of Anatomy, University of Hong Kong. These same kinds of physical restrictions are now being applied at the senior secondary level as well *(Renmin ribao,* 18 June 1981; and the printed list of the Guangdong Provincial Keypoint Middle School Enrollment Health Regulations, obtained by Prof. Peter Mauger in the spring of 1982).

14. Based on interview files for Fudan (pp. 48, 50, 56) and Shandong (p. 13); and two lists of the main specialty qualifications in *Guangming ribao,* 13 July 1979, and in *Gaokao zhinan* [Guide to the college entrance examinations], ed. Hubeisheng zhongxiaoxue jiaoxue jiaocai yanjiushi (Hubei: Hubei renmin chubanshe, May 1979), pp. 284-86.

15. *Nanfang ribao,* 29 October 1981.

16. *Wenhuibao* (Shanghai), 21 August 1980.

17. *Zhongguo qingnian bao,* 5 August 1980.

18. *Wenhuibao* (Shanghai), 4 January 1981; *Guangming ribao,* 26 November 1981; *Renmin ribao,* 2 and 3 June 1980, 28 April 1981, and 14 March 1982; and *South China Morning Post,* Agence France Presse, Beijing, 2 November 1983.

19. According to a statement made at China's First National Symposium on the Dissemination of Eugenic Knowledge, as reported in Xinhua-English (Beijing), 4 November 1981, in *Xinhua News Bulletin,* 5 November 1981.

20. "1981 College Enrollment Work Regulations," *State Council Bulletin,* no. 4 (25 April 1981), p. 122; and Zhao Sheng, "Answering Readers' Questions," *Renmin jiaoyu,* no. 3 (1981), p. 10.

21. These national physical fitness standards are reprinted in *Yijiuqiwu zhonggong nianbao* [1975 yearbook on Chinese communism] (Taibei: Zonggong yanjiu zazhishi, 1975), pp. ii, 192-94.

22. See, for example, *Wenhuibao* (Shanghai), 11 May 1980.

23. See, for example, the 1981 announcement of the colleges and universities enrolling in Shanghai *(Wenhuibao,* 15 May 1981).

24. *Wenhuibao* (Shanghai), 6 June 1980 and 15 May 1981; *Beijing ribao,* 28 May 1980 and 19 May 1981.

25. *Zhejiang ribao,* 8 July and 1 August 1981.

26. Interview files: Zhongshan University, pp. 18, 20; and Shandong University, pp. 13-14.

27. Nanjing University file, p. 78; *Xinhua ribao* (Nanjing), 2 August 1980 and 9 July 1981; *Tianjin ribao,* 12 July 1981.

28. Interview files: Zhongshan, p. 20; East China Teachers' Training, p. 34; and Nankai, p. 11.

29. See, for example: *Guangming ribao,* 31 March 1981; *Wenhuibao* (Shanghai), 16 April 1981 and 29 July 1979; *Zhongguo qingnian bao,* 2 August 1979.

30. *Xinhua ribao,* (Nanjing), 9 July 1981.

31. *Tianjin ribao,* 16 July 1981.

32. *Tianjin ribao,* 12 July 1981.

33. Interview files: Fudan, pp. 51, 53-54, 57; Nanjing, p. 22; Zhongshan, pp. 19-20; and *Guangming ribao,* 13 June 1980.

34. *Guangzhou ribao*, 18 August 1981; administrators indicated that such changes in preference are common.

35. *Wenhuibao* (Shanghai), 25 May 1981.

36. *Tianjin ribao*, 12 July 1980.

37. "Yijiubasannian quanrizhi gaodeng xuexiao zhaokao xinshengde guiding" [1983 regulations governing the entrance examinations for full-day institutions of higher learning], *State Council Bulletin*, no. 7 (10 May 1983), p. 249.

Chapter IV

1. This basic information concerning the entrance examinations is published each year in the *State Council Bulletin* as well as in the national and local press; see, for example, *Guangming ribao*, 16 March 1981 and 17 March 1983; *Beijing ribao*, 17 May 1980 and 15 May 1981; *Nanfang ribao* (Guangzhou), 11 May 1980 and 27 March 1981.

2. Li Shuxi and Chen Hao, "The Development of the 1981 College Entrance Exam Questions," *Renmin jiaoyu*, no. 8 (1981), pp. 37, 39, 40; and *Guangming ribao*, 9 and 16 August 1981.

3. *Zhejiang ribao*, 28 July 1980.

4. Interview files: Jilin, p. 17; Nanjing, p. 75; Wuhan, p. 59; Nankai, p. 10; Fudan, p. 45; Chinese People's University, p. 4; Shandong, p. 10; Zhongshan, p. 21.

5. The 1978 examinations are translated and analyzed along with the 1978 review outline in Barendsen, ed., *The 1978 National College Entrance Examination*. All of the math, physics, and chemistry examinations from 1949-78 period are reprinted in *Zhongguo daxue ruxue shiti tijie huibian: shuxue, wuli, huaxue bufen, 1949-1978* [A collection of questions and solutions for the Chinese university entrance examinations in mathematics, physics and chemistry, 1949-1978] (Hong Kong: Xiandaihua chubanshe, 1978). One edition of the 1980 examinations in all subjects also contains the back-up questions: *Tongyi zhaosheng shiti he jieda* [Unified enrollment questions and answers] (Shanghai: Shanghai kexue jishu chubanshe, 1981).

6. *Wenhuibao* (Shanghai), 15 July 1980; *Tianjin ribao*, 10 July 1980; *Zhongguo qingnian bao*, 26 July 1980.

7. Interview files: East China Teachers' Training University, pp. 30, 33; Nanjing, p. 75, 77; Shandong, pp. 11-12; Lanzhou, p. 3; Jilin, p. 18. See also *Tianjin ribao*, 5 and 10 July 1980; *Zhejiang ribao*, 28 July 1980; *Zhongguo qingnian bao*, 26 July 1980; *Beijing ribao*, 28 July 1981; *Guangming ribao*, 29 July 1981; *Nanfang ribao*, 24 July 1981.

8. *Guangming ribao*, 3 August 1979; *Zhejiang ribao*, 28 July 1980; "Jiaoyubu guanyu yijiubaling nian quanguo gaodeng xuexiao zhaosheng gongzuo huiyide baogao" [Education Ministry report on the 1980 national college enrollment work conference] (10 April 1980), *State Council Bulletin*, no. 5 (23 June 1980), p. 160.

9. *Zhejiang ribao*, 1 August 1980.

10. Interview files: Shandong, pp. 8-9; Lanzhou, p. 4; Nanjing, p. 77; Jilin, p. 18; Zhongshan, p. 18; and *Zhejiang ribao*, 1 August 1980.

11. *Tianjin ribao*, 3 and 19 August 1980.

12. Huang Xinbai (Vice-Minister of Education), "Wenbu gaige gaoxiao tongkao zhaosheng zhidu" [Steadily reform the unified examination enrollment system for institutions of higher learning], *Renmin jiaoyu*, no. 3 (1981), p. 6.

13. Interview files: Shandong, p. 8; Nanjing, p. 77; Wuhan, p. 60.

14. Xinhua-English (Beijing), 27 September 1979, in *Xinhua News Bulletin*, 28 September 1979.

15. Huang Xinbai, "Steadily Reform the Unified Examination System," p. 6.

16. *Zhejiang ribao*, 16 August 1981.

17. *Zhongguo qingnian bao*, 5 August 1980; *Sichuan ribao*, 11 August 1981.
18. *Zhongguo qingnian bao*, 5 August 1980; *Wenhuibao* (Shanghai), 3 and 21 June 1980.
19. *Beijing ribao*, 27 August 1981; *Tianjin ribao*, 30 July 1981.
20. *Guangming ribao*, 16 August 1981.
21. *Beijing ribao*, 1 and 27 August 1981.
22. See *Wenzhaibao*, no. 45 (10 August 1982), p. 1.
23. *Guangming ribao*, 5 August 1980.
24. Nanjing University file, p. 83.
25. Zhao Sheng, "Answering Readers' Questions on this Year's Enrollment to Institutions of Higher Learning," *Renmin jiaoyu*, no. 3 (1981), p. 10.
26. Ibid., and "1980 College Enrollment Work Regulations," *State Council Bulletin*, no. 5 (23 June 1980), p. 164; "1981 College Enrollment Work Regulations," *State Council Bulletin*, no. 4 (25 April 1981), p. 122.

Chapter V

1. "1981 College Enrollment Work Regulations," *State Council Bulletin*, no. 4 (25 April 1981), p. 121.
2. The first-category institutions are listed in the national enrollment regulations; see *State Council Bulletin*, no. 5 (23 June 1980), p. 164; no. 4 (25 April 1981), p. 122; and no. 7 (10 May 1983), p. 250.
3. *Nanfang ribao*, 9 August 1981.
4. *Xinhua ribao* (Nanjing), 31 July 1981.
5. *Zhejiang ribao*, 1 August 1981.
6. *Tianjin ribao*, 3 and 23 August and 6 September 1980.
7. Huang Xinbai, "Steadily Reform the Unified Examination Enrollment System for Institutions of Higher Learning," *Renmin jiaoyu*, no. 3 (1981), p. 6.
8. *Tianjin ribao*, 19 August 1980; *Zhejiang ribao*, 16 August 1981.
9. *Zhejiang ribao*, 16 August 1981.
10. *Sichuan ribao*, 11 August 1981.
11. *Dazhong ribao*, 2 August 1981.
12. *Zhejiang ribao*, 1 August 1980.
13. Nankai University file, p. 13.
14. *Sichuan ribao*, 11 and 24 August 1981.
15. *Guangming ribao*, 5 November 1981.
16. Interview files: Nanjing, p. 82; Wuhan, p. 64; Shandong, p. 17.
17. Fudan University file, pp. 51, 53.
18. Shandong University file, pp. 15, 17.
19. Fudan University file, pp. 52-53, 55.
20. Wuhan University file, pp. 59, 61.
21. East China Teachers' Training University file, p. 32.
22. *Wenhuibao* (Shanghai), 9 August 1980.
23. *Xinhua ribao* (Nanjing), 3 September 1981.
24. *Sichuan ribao*, 21 August 1981.

25. *Tianjin ribao*, 3 August 1980. The difference was reduced to five points the following year (*Tianjin ribao*, 30 July 1981). For official recognition of this problem, see, *Renmin ribao*, 8 March 1981, and Beijing radio, 23 October 1980, in SWB, FE/6563/BII/6, 31 October 1980.

26. Xinhua-English (Beijing), 13 June 1978, in FBIS, 15 June 1978, p. E-5; Xinhua-English (Beijing), 16 May 1979, in FBIS, 17 May 1979, p. L-17; and the national enrollment regulations: *State Council Bulletin*, no. 5 (23 June 1980), p. 164, and no. 7 (10 May 1983), p. 249.

27. *Sichuan ribao*, 11 August 1981.

28. Shandong University file, p. 16.

29. Zhongshan University file, p. 21.

30. *Guangzhou ribao*, 29 July 1981.

31. Nanjing University file, p. 81.

32. East China Teachers' Training University file, p. 32.

33. Fudan University file, p. 51.

34. *Wenhuibao* (Shanghai), 14 October 1980.

35. Wuhan University file, pp. 59-60, 64.

36. Lanzhou University file, pp. 4-5.

37. The ten minorities institutes are: the Central National Minorities Institute (Beijing), the Northwest National Minorities Institute (Lanzhou), the Southwest National Minorities Institute (Chengdu), the Central South National Minorities Institute (Wuhan), the Guizhou National Minorities Institute (Guiyang), the Yunnan National Minorities Institute (Kunming), the Guangxi National Minorities Institute (Nanning), the Qinghai National Minorities Institute (Xining), the Tibetan National Minorities Institute (Xianyang, Shaanxi), and the Guangdong National Minorities Institute (Hainan Island), according to *Guangxi minzu xueyuan xuebao* [Journal of the Guangxi Minorities Institute], no. 1 (1981), p. 130. My thanks to John Dolfin for directing me to this source.

38. *Beijing Review*, no. 9 (1980), p. 17.

39. Northwest National Minorities Institute notes, p. 3.

40. *Sichuan ribao*, 21 August 1981.

41. *Sichuan ribao*, 11 August 1981.

42. These fixed patterns of university life and the problems they pose are discussed in my first "China's Universities" research report (*Modern China*, April 1982). On China's need for more tertiary-level students, see Song Jian, "Population and Education," *Journal of the Dialectics of Nature*, no. 3 (June 1980), in JPRS/77745/3 April 1981/PSM/178, pp. 43-47.

43. *Guangming ribao*, 3 March 1978.

44. Interview files: Beijing Teachers' Training University, p. 4; Wuhan, p. 11; Shandong, pp. 5, 76; Zhongshan, p. 11; Xiamen, p. 16; Fudan, p. 7.

45. *Wenhuibao* (Shanghai), 27 July, 2 August, and 4 September 1980.

46. *Guangming ribao*, 18 October 1980.

47. *Zhejiang ribao*, 18 September 1980; *Guangming ribao*, 30 May, 3 June, 29 August, 21 September, and 23 November 1980.

48. *Guangming ribao*, 14 June 1980.

49. *Guangming ribao*, 14 June 1980; *Zhongguo qingnian bao*, 23 September 1980.

50. *Guangming ribao*, 5 September, and 4 and 18 October 1980.

Chapter VI

1. For a full account of these policies, see Robert Taylor, *China's Intellectual Dilemma: Politics and University Enrollment, 1949-1978.*
2. Suzanne Pepper, "Chinese Education after Mao," *The China Quarterly*, no. 81 (March 1980), p. 63.
3. *Renmin ribao*, 12 May 1978.
4. *Zhongguo baike nianjian, 1980*, p. 538.
5. *Zhongguo jingji nianjian, 1981*, p. IV-204.
6. This last quote appeared in the press in a reader's letter of complaint (*Guangzhou ribao*, 24 June 1981). All others are from interviews.
7. See Stephen Jay Gould, *The Mismeasure of Man* (New York: W. W. Norton, 1981), especially the section on "Women's Brains," pp. 103-7.
8. Two articles in *Jiaoyu yanjiu* [Education research], no. 12 (1981), the journal of the Central Educational Science Research Institute in Beijing, elaborated on the differences in intelligence between the sexes. Fu Anqiu from the Zhejiang Teachers' Training College summarized the difference as follows: "With respect to their thought capabilities (*siwei nengli*), the experiential mentality is higher in women; a narrated event carries deep emotional coloring for them; and they are inclined to think in terms of images. But women in their behavior are easily influenced by suggestion; lack decisiveness; are sensitive to difficulties; are prone to stick to conventions; and are easily inhibited by new things or doubts about things. Women therefore generally prefer to study such subjects as Chinese (language and literature), foreign languages, history, geography, and biology. The thinking of men is characterized by expansiveness, quick-wittedness, and creativity. Their ability to generalize problems is comparatively stronger; they like to manipulate matter and probe its causes; they are inclined to logical thought. They therefore generally prefer such subjects as math, physics, and chemistry." The author suggests that biological reasons should not be overlooked in seeking the causes of these intellectual differences—which can, nevertheless, be modified through education. Though noting that it has not yet been conclusively proven, the author asserts that the intellectual differences between the sexes "are related to different genetically determined chromosomes between men and women; to differences in the functions of the two sides of the brain; and to the influence of hormonal differences on the composition of the brain." ("Zhili fazhande xingbie tezheng yu jiaoyu" [Sexual characteristics of intellectual development and their relation to education], p. 39.)

   The second article, by Zeng Jinghua of the Guilin Municipal Education Bureau, states that by comparison with women, and despite some exceptions among them, "in general, men's knowledge is more extensive, their imaginative capabilities are richer, their thought capabilities are stronger, and their special capabilities are greater." The main reasons are: first, physiological; second, the feudal or historical tradition of favoring men; and third, the objective influences of capitalist thought. The physiological reasons advanced here are all related to the hormonal imbalances of adolescence which have a greater influence on girls at that age. The author referred specifically to the fluctuations in pulse rate, blood pressure, breathing, body temperature, muscular function, and eyesight during menstruation. The physical discomfort all of this causes is said to be accompanied by much emotional stress. With the ensuing "development of sexual awareness and enhanced sense of shame among girl students, the scope of their daily activities lessens. Hence, their studies are influenced in many ways and it is difficult to avoid some decline in their scholastic achievement." ("Zhongxue nannushengde chayi yu jiaoyu" [Differences between boy and girl students in middle school and their relevance to education], p. 44.)
9. *Beijing ribao*, 27 August 1981.

Chapter VII

1. Huang Xinbai, "Steadily Reform the Unified Examination Enrollment System for Institutions of Higher Learning," *Renmin jiaoyu*, no. 3 (1981), p. 27.
2. *Guangming ribao*, 4 August 1981; and *Beijing ribao*, 7 May 1980.
3. *Guangming ribao*, 19 May 1978; *Wenhuibao* (Shanghai), 27 March 1980; "1981 College Enrollment Work Regulations," *State Council Bulletin*, no. 4 (25 April 1981), p. 122.
4. Zhao Sheng, "Answering Readers' Questions on This Year's Enrollment to Institutions of Higher Learning," *Renmin jiaoyu*, no. 3 (1981), p. 9.
5. Huang Xinbai, "Steadily Reform the Unified Examination Enrollment System," p. 6.

GLOSSARY

ban 班

banzhuren 班主任

baoming gaokao 报名高考

baozheng zhiliang 保证质量

benke 本科

benren chengfen 本人成份

biye jianding 毕业鉴定

biyesheng dengjibiao 毕业生登记表

buxiban 补习班

caiwuchu 财务处

chengfen 成份

cuoshi 措施

dang'an zhidu 档案制度

danyihua 单一化

dazhuan 大专

diaodang fenshuxian 调档分数线

dingxiang fenpai 定向分配

dingxiang zhaosheng 定向招生

fangkuang 放宽

fenshuduan 分数段

fucha 复查

fushu zhongxue 附属中学

fuzhong xuexiao 附中学校

ganbu 干部

gaodeng zhuanke 高等专科

gaokao fuxi 高考复习

geming ganbu 革命干部

gongren 工人

gongshangye 工商业

guagou 挂钩

guangrong 光荣

gugan fenzi 骨干分子

guojia tiyu duanlian biaozhun 国家体育锻炼标准

huaqing jiexian 划清界线

huo 活

jiangdi 降低

jiangdi fenshu 降低分数

jianli 简历

jianzi 尖子

jianzi xuesheng 尖子学生

jianziban 尖子班
jiaocha 较差
jiaowuchu 教务处
jiaoyu xueyuan 教育学院
jiating chushen 家庭出身
jiating zhuyao chengyuan 家庭主要成員
jiben jianshechu 基本建设处
jimi 机密
jishu gongren 技术工人
jiti beike 集体备课
juemi 绝密
kaochang 考场
kexue yanjiuchu 科学研究处
lengmen 冷门
li-ke 理科
luqu 録取
miji 密级
mishu 秘书
nongye 农业
peiyang rencai 培养人才
pingjuan weiyuanhui 评卷委员会
puji 普及
putonghua 普通话
remen 热门
renshichu 人事处
shelai shequ 社来社去
sheng gaoxiao zhaosheng weiyuanhui 省高校招生委员会
shengchan jishu jiaoyu 生产技术教育
shengxuelu 升学率
shenti 身体
shenti jiancha 身体检查
sheyuan 社员
si 死
siwei nengli 思维能力
songdang fenshuxian 送档分数线
tiaoming'e 调名额
tijianxian 体检线
tushuguan 图书馆
waishi bangongshi 外事办公室
wen-ke 文科
xianshen 献身
xiaoshang 小商
xiaoshougongyezhe 小手工业者
xiaozhang bangongshi 校长办公室
xiongdi 兄弟

xuanze yudi 选择余地

xueshengke 学生科

xueyuan 学院

yanjiushengke 研究生科

yincai shijiao 因材施教

youxuan 优选

youxuan luqu 优选录取

yukao 预考

zeyou luqu 择优录取

zeyou zhaogu 择优照顾

zhaogu 照顾

zhengzhi mianmu 政治面目

zhengzhi shencha 政治审查

zhili 智力

zhiliang jiancha 质量验查

zhiye 职业

zhiye jishu zhongxue 职业技术中学

zhiye xuexiao 职业学校

zhiyuan 职员

zhiyuanbiao 志愿表

zhongdeng zhuanye xuexiao 中等专业学校

zhongdian 重点

zhongxin 中心

zhongzhuan 中专

zhuanke 专科

zhuanke xuexiao 专科学校

zhuanye 专业

zhunkaozheng 准考证

zhuyao shehui guanxi 主要社会关係

zonghexing daxue 综合性大学

zongwuchu 总务处

zuidi luqu fenshuxian 最低录取分数线

MICHIGAN MONOGRAPHS IN CHINESE STUDIES

No. 2. *The Cultural Revolution: 1967 in Review*, four essays by Michel Oksenberg, Carl Riskin, Robert Scalapino, and Ezra Vogel.

No. 3. *Two Studies in Chinese Literature*, by Li Chi and Dale Johnson.

Early Communist China: Two Studies, by Ronald Suleski and Daniel Bays.

No. 5. *The Chinese Economy, ca. 1870-1911*, by Albert Feuerwerker.

No. 7. *The Treaty Ports and China's Modernization: What Went Wrong?*, by Rhoads Murphey.

No. 8. *Two Twelfth Century Texts on Chinese Painting*, by Robert J. Maeda.

No. 10. *Educated Youth and the Cultural Revolution in China*, by Martin Singer.

No. 11. *Premodern China: A Bibliographical Introduction*, by Chun-shu Chang.

No. 12. *Two Studies on Ming History*, by Charles O. Hucker.

No. 13. *Nineteenth-Century China: Five Imperialist Perspectives*, selected by Dilip Basu and edited by Rhoads Murphey.

No. 14. *Modern China, 1840-1972: An Introduction to Sources and Research Aids*, by Andrew J. Nathan.

No. 15. *Women in China: Studies in Social Change and Feminism*, edited by Marilyn B. Young.

No. 17. *China's Allocation of Fixed Capital Investment, 1952-1957*, by Chu-yuan Cheng.

No. 18. *Health, Conflict, and the Chinese Political System*, by David M. Lampton.

No. 19. *Chinese and Japanese Music-Dramas*, edited by J. I. Crump and William P. Malm.

No. 21. *Rebellion in Nineteenth-Century China*, by Albert Feuerwerker.

No. 22. *Between Two Plenums: China's Intraleadership Conflict, 1959-1962*, by Ellis Joffe.

No. 23. *"Proletarian Hegemony" in the Chinese Revolution and the Canton Commune of 1927*, by S. Bernard Thomas.

No. 24. *Chinese Communist Materials at the Bureau of Investigation Archives, Taiwan*, by Peter Donovan, Carl E. Dorris, and Lawrence R. Sullivan.

No. 25. *Shanghai's Old-Style Banks (Ch'ien-chuang), 1800-1935*, by Andrea Lee McElderry.

No. 26. *The Sian Incident: A Pivotal Point in Modern Chinese History*, by Tien-wei Wu.

No. 27. *State and Society in Eighteenth-Century China: The Ch'ing Empire in Its Glory*, by Albert Feuerwerker.

No. 28. *Intellectual Ferment for Political Reforms in Taiwan, 1971-1973*, by Mab Huang.

No. 29. *The Foreign Establishment in China in the Early Twentieth Century*, by Albert Feuerwerker.

No. 30. *A Translation of Lao Tzu's* Tao Te Ching *and Wang Pi's Commentary*, by Paul J. Lin.

No. 31. *Economic Trends in the Republic of China, 1912-1949*, by Albert Feuerwerker.

No. 33. *Central Documents and Politburo Politics in China*, by Kenneth Lieberthal.

No. 34. *The Ming Dynasty: Its Origins and Evolving Institutions*, by Charles O. Hucker.

No. 35. *Double Jeopardy: A Critique of Seven Yuan Courtroom Dramas*, by Ching-hsi Perng.

No. 36. *Chinese Domestic Politics and Foreign Policy in the 1970s*, by Allen S. Whiting.

No. 37. *Shanghai, 1925: Urban Nationalism and the Defense of Foreign Privilege*, by Nicholas R. Clifford.

No. 38. *Voices from Afar: Modern Chinese Writers on Oppressed Peoples and Their Literature*, by Irene Eber.

No. 39. *Mao Zedong's "Talks at the Yan'an Conference on Literature and Art": A Translation of the 1943 Text with Commentary*, by Bonnie S. McDougall.

No. 40. *Yuarn Music Dramas: Studies in Prosody and Structure and a Complete Catalogue of Northern Arias in the Dramatic Style*, by Dale R. Johnson.

No. 41. *Proclaiming Harmony*, translated by William O. Hennessey.

No. 42. *A Song for One or Two: Music and the Concept of Art in Early China*, by Kenneth DeWoskin.

No. 43. *The Economic Development of Manchuria: The Rise of a Frontier Economy*, by Kang Chao.

No. 44. *A Bibliography of Chinese-Language Materials on the People's Communes*, by Wei-yi Ma.

No. 45. *Chinese Social and Economic History from the Song to 1900*, edited by Albert Feuerwerker.

No. 46. *China's Universities: Post-Mao Enrollment Policies and Their Impact on the Structure of Secondary Education*, by Suzanne Pepper.

No. 47. *Songs from Xanadu*, by J. I. Crump.

No. 48. *Social Organization in South China, 1911-1949: The Case of The Kuan Lineage of K'ai-p'ing County*, by Yuen-fong Woon.

No. 49. *Labor and the Chinese Revolution*, by S. Bernard Thomas (cloth only).

No. 50. *Soviet Studies of Premodern China: Assessments of Recent Scholarship*, edited by Gilbert Rozman.

No. 51. *Career Patterns in the Ch'ing Dynasty: The Office of the Governor-General*, by Raymond W. Chu and William G. Saywell.

MICHIGAN ABSTRACTS OF CHINESE AND JAPANESE WORKS ON CHINESE HISTORY

No. 1. *The Ming Tribute Grain System*, by Hoshi Ayao, translated by Mark Elvin.

No. 2. *Commerce and Society in Sung China*, by Shiba Yoshinobu, translated by Mark Elvin.

No. 3. *Transport in Transition: The Evolution of Traditional Shipping In China*, translated by Andrew Watson.

No. 4. *Japanese Perspectives on China's Early Modernization: A Bibliographical Survey*, by K. M. Kim.

No. 5. *The Silk Industry in Ch'ing China*, by Shih Min-hsiung, translated by E-tu Zen Sun.

No. 6. *The Pawnshop in China*, by T. S. Whelan.

Michigan Papers and Abstracts available from:

Center for Chinese Studies
The University of Michigan
104 Lane Hall (Publications)
Ann Arbor, Michigan 48109 USA